1.50

The *real*

Maria

"After reading this heart-warming account of her life we realize that in this famous woman lies a goodness and greatness found only in those who recognize the will of God in all things and accept it graciously."

Family Digest

"Here in her own words is the story of her life, recounted in such a way that you can almost hear her speak. Part of the book's charm is Maria's honest report of her shortcomings as well as her triumphs . . . Fascinating!"

Christian Life

Maria

Maria von Trapp

AVON
PUBLISHERS OF BARD, CAMELOT, DISCUS, EQUINOX AND FLARE BOOKS

AVON BOOKS
A division of
The Hearst Corporation
959 Eighth Avenue
New York, New York 10019

Copyright © 1972 by Creation House.
Published by arrangement with Creation House, Inc.
Library of Congress Catalogue Card Number: 72-81112.

ISBN: 0-380-00783-5

First Avon Printing, December, 1973.
Eighth Printing

AVON TRADEMARK REG. U.S. PAT. OFF. AND
FOREIGN COUNTRIES, REGISTERED TRADEMARK—
MARCA REGISTRADA, HECHO EN CHICAGO, U.S.A.

Printed in the U.S.A.

I dedicate this book

to the One

who made the name

MARIA

famous for all time

CONTENTS

Maria

1

Learning to Love

Not long ago I realized: The past I cannot shut out. It came about—of all times—during a lecture tour that had taken me to Salt Lake City, Utah. I was scheduled to speak at the Mormon Church University.

A Morman bishop drove me twenty miles from Salt Lake City through the mountains of Utah.

"You know," he said, "we are coming close to the exams of the midyear."

"Aha," I acknowledged.

"Our lecture series is not compulsory. The students do not have to attend."

"So?" I answered, not knowing what he was hinting at.

"We have booked you in the fieldhouse," he informed me.

"And what is a fieldhouse?" I asked.

After a little hesitation he informed me it was their big stadium which held 14,000 people.

Now I understood. "Bishop," I said, "if you are worried that we might have only a small audience on account of the exams, all I ask is that you transfer my lecture from the fieldhouse into a classroom so I can see my audience, and everything will be all right."

The bishop was visibly relieved.

At that time we were just nearing the campus. I could see the buildings already, but what was that?

13

Groups of students were milling around and I could hear shouting. Then I saw a look of real apprehension on the face of my driver. Only the week before the UCLA campus at Berkeley had suffered under the first student riots. The bishop asked me to wait in the car while he investigated the noise.

In no time he was back with a big smile. The students were fighting to get into the fieldhouse which had been filled to capacity for over half an hour already, and he had to raise the ban of no one being allowed to stand in the aisles so that they could all get in.

Then came a really wonderful hour together with these young people who listened in rapt attention to my story. After the last word of my speech there was thundering applause, and the first standing ovation since President Kennedy had spoken in this fieldhouse.

And then came a question-and-answer period. These young people had obviously listened not only with their heads, but also with their hearts, and most pertinent questions came forth. Just as the bell rang, indicating the end of the period, one timid hand was raised in the front row and I decided this would be the last question.

A tall, very pale, bespectacled youth got up and said, "Mrs. von Trapp, you come from a large family, don't you? You must have had a very happy childhood."

For an instant I hesitated. I really hated to disappoint him, but I had to answer truthfully.

"No, I am sorry, I was an only child and an orphan, and I had a most unhappy childhood."

At that, my young philosopher frowned and, after a short hesitancy, announced, "I am studying psychology and, according to the book, you should have become a juvenile delinquent."

14

This brought down the house.

After a very pleasant lunch I was driven back to Salt Lake City by two students. At the beginning of my return trip I excused myself for having a light headache and being a little tired. This was perfectly true, but I was also deeply stirred up by that boy's last remark.

Little did he know how close he had come to the truth. My thoughts were carried back to the beginning—

* * *

I never knew my mother, and I only knew my father very little. By pasting together bits of information which I heard at different times, I learned that he was a really tragic figure. I knew that when my father had been a young man in Vienna, he fell in love with a beautiful girl from Tirol, married her, and after a year they were the happy and proud parents of a little boy named Karl. During the early summer, when mother and child were ready to travel again, my father took them home to her family to show off the little prince. And then he invited his young wife to take a trip with horse and buggy. My father was holding the reins as they drove beside one of those wild mountain brooks found in the Alps. They were passing a tremendous waterfall—a sight to behold—when my father turned onto a small narrow bridge over the falls. The young horse shied, throwing them both over the railing, and my father had to watch helplessly as his young wife, who could not swim, was hurled down the falls. The thundering noise swallowed up her cries for help.

As he returned to his wife's home, he was a broken man. He took his ten-week-old son with him to Vienna, where he asked an elderly cousin to take care of him.

And then my father disappeared. From time to time money orders came from different corners of the earth —the first from Arabia, several from India, others from places the people had never heard of, and some from the South Seas. For a while they came from Japan; then, after a long pause, there was one from Turkey. But never a return address. Only money.

Young Karl grew from babyhood into a boy. After finishing high school he went to a technical institute and became an engineer. But by now a strange bitterness had taken hold of this young man; he did not want any personal relations, he told his foster mother, with the man who had no use for him when he needed him most. This estrangement never ceased.

Soon after my father's return to Vienna he made a trip to his wife's home to visit her grave. To his great astonishment he found there a beautiful young girl looking strikingly similar to his beloved Clara. This one was named Augusta and called Gusti. My father was completely dumbfounded. For him it was like a greeting from beyond the grave, and he would have liked to marry her on the spot. He did marry her at his earliest convenience and just as soon as they allowed him to, and young Gusti, age eighteen, went with her husband to Vienna.

There they lived "happily ever after" until in due time a baby announced its coming. I was told that my mother was very homesick in Vienna, as all people from Tirol always are, yearning for the mountains. So she begged her husband, "Let's go home for Christmas, please."

And so they did. Right after Christmas he had to return to his business but he allowed her to stay a little longer, but he made her promise to come to Vienna in due time to have the baby born there.

A few weeks passed and then my mother counted

16

on her fingers that the time would come soon, so she obediently boarded a train. But the baby in question (being me, and showing my true nature of being impetuous even then) couldn't wait. In the night before the 26th of January—before midnight!—I was born on the train. The train was almost empty. The conductor, having nine children of his own, knew all about everything and assisted my mother most professionally. But then he was stuck. He tried all his power of persuasion to get the young lady out of the train and into a hospital bed, which she refused sternly.

"I promised my husband to arrive on this train, and he will be waiting for me at the station in Vienna. And there I will arrive" was her answer.

And so it happened, to my chagrin, that when my mother appeared with the finished product and I was taken by her anxious husband to the General Hospital in Vienna—"just in case"—they wrote on my baptism certificate that I was born on January 26 in Vienna instead of "on the train in Tirol on January 25."

As much as I could find out, my mother and father were very happy together and I grew up into a healthy youngster.

I had walked very early and was running around fast as a weasel, but I hadn't said a single word yet and I was already two years old when my anxious parents took me to a doctor. He took one good look at me, shook his head, and said, "Don't worry. She will make up for this later." (Once in a while I have been reminded of this prediction.)

And then disaster struck again. My young mother caught pneumonia and, this being before the time of antibiotics, no doctor could help her. I was told that my father thought that if he held her upright, leaning against his shoulder, she simply could not die. And so she died, leaning on his heart.

17

Again the poor man was left with a helpless little child. In his own arms he brought me to the same cousin who had brought up my brother and who was in her sixties by now. But she took me in most willingly and lovingly.

My first memories go back to the little house on the outskirts of Vienna, a section which had just been incorporated into the big city but was really still a village with its long main village street. There the farmhouses, low stone buildings with just a ground floor, were strung together by big tall wooden gates through which the hay wagons passed. Soon I would be "big" enough to go to one farmer for the daily milk and to another one to get the potatoes, and a third one for vegetables; and so I came to know them all. Every farm and every house had its own well from which the people had drunk from since time immemorial; but since our village was now part of Vienna, we were told not to use well water for drinking anymore, only for cooking or washing. Therefore, everyday at 5 P.M. I was sent to the city spring to bring home two milk pitchers full of water from the Vienna Woods. This section of Vienna borders the Marchfeld, a wide stretched-out plain, very flat, but full of historic memories. There I spent my early childhood.

My foster mother was very kind, as was my foster father who died when I was very young; I remember his funeral only dimly.

The only family I knew as a child were my foster parents, two grown-up sons, Alfred and Pepi, and two grown-up daughters, Anni and Kathy. Alfred worked as an engineer in a very distant part of Austria which now belongs to Czechoslovakia. Pepi went to the University in Vienna and became a doctor of linguistics. Later he worked in the government department of education, where he rose to a very high position. Anni

18

worked as a secretary and was away all day. Kathy was busy around the house. Soon after her father's death, Anni married a judge, who also made his way high up in the justice department. Also, Pepi married; his brother-in-law, known to me as Uncle Fritz, was my puppy love. He visited us only rarely. Although he was twenty-five years older than I, my young heart was fluttering because he was, oh, so beautiful.

Unfortunately it was not the custom that I go visiting to other homes with children or that I would be allowed to invite children to our home. It was so very much a home of grownups set in their ways; they obviously didn't want to be disturbed by the noise of children, but I'm sure there were no hard feelings. It simply wasn't done, but the fact is that I grew up a very lonesome child. Kathy accompanied me every day to school and picked me up again afterward, so even there I didn't have the company of the other girls chatting and playing with each other. And so it happened that out of necessity I began to invent company for myself. I imagined that I was living with a large family named Paultraxl; there were a mother, father and eleven children. Mr. Paultraxl was a well-to-do farmer, and through him I learned the most minute details of what was going on in the barn and in the field. It didn't matter that I had actually read all his books; in my make-believe life I was being told these things by Paultraxl. His wife was a loving soul, jolly, full of fun, hugging and kissing me, and all their children were lots of fun. Once in a great while Mrs. Paultraxl's sister, Frau Irbinger, came visiting with her clan. My, was that an ado. It so happened that this took place when my own family was out visiting, which was very rarely, because I needed all the space to accommodate my guests. If my foster family came home unexpectedly, they found all the chairs which we owned from all the rooms grouped around in a circle, as I had to take care of all my company. They would find me happily chatting, going from chair to chair, offering make-believe food and drink. Many a time I was scolded harshly for all that nonsense and my otherwise-kind foster mother would say, "Don't you ever let me see that again."

So I was pushed back with my whole world of make believe into the distant corners of the garden. There I had made up practically an entire bakery with my little tin cake forms and the sand pile providing *Gulgelhupf,* and all kinds of lush Viennese cakes like *Linzertorte, Apfelstrudel* and *Sachertorte.* I had them all lined up, preparing food for the "next visit."

In these first years of my childhood, God entered my life for the first time in a very gentle and loving way. My foster mother was a deeply religious person, truly pious. Every morning she would go to church, many times taking me with her, and I remember how I often looked at her rather than at the altar. Her face radiated kindliness and the love of God.

At home she would sometimes take me on her lap in the evening and go through an illustrated Bible in large print. I am sure I would think the pictures atrocious now, but at that time they were a source of great happiness. I remember a child Jesus in a pink gown with yellow curls, His mother all dressed in blue. I couldn't get enough of it. And then at the gruesome pictures of our Lord's passion, my little heart welled up in pity and misery. Once my foster mother found me in a corner curled up over the Bible as I pierced the eyes of those bad men torturing our dear Lord— with a crochet hook.

My foster mother told me the basic truths: That God is everywhere and sees me always; I can't hide

20

from Him. Even if human eyes don't see that I do something wrong, He sees it.

That He is a loving Father who is sad if I am bad and who is happy if I am good.

That my guardian angel is always with me, watching over me, warning me. And she taught me a little prayer which I had to add to my morning prayer.

That Mary was my loving mother, especially as my true mother had left me too early, and I should always turn to her if I was in trouble.

So I was finally one of the white-clad little girls who made their first communion in the third grade. I resolved on that day that I would never, but really never, again offend God, to whom I wanted to belong till I died.

The real highlights of these years were the meetings with my father. But they were not normal meetings of a five- or six- or seven-year-old with an elderly father who might take her on his lap and tell her stories. No, it was altogether different. My father could not adjust any longer to the life of an engineer. Something was broken in him. He could not continue a plain ordinary life like any of his colleagues. When he returned from those many years of absence, I was told he came back knowing how to speak and write in fourteen languages. He returned with cases and cases of books and instruments. Taking a large apartment in a very good section of Vienna, he filled the rooms with his books so that you couldn't see the original color of the wallpaper anywhere. He turned one room into an aviary where the doorframe was covered with a net. Inside was a little girl's paradise: birds of all colors and sizes, really all colors of the rainbow, fluttering happily around. Some of them were even nesting in the twigs of a big tree which was put in the middle of the room.

All of them were tweeting and singing happily. They were the joy and pride of my father.

In all the corners of the other rooms were instruments of all sizes and shapes. Some were from the viol family—from the biggest bass cello, eight feet long, down to the small ones two feet long. Then in another corner were flutes of all sizes and shapes. Then came the weirdest-looking brass instruments. And in order to entertain his young guest, my father would perch on the edge of a table and grab one or the other and play fluently, but sometimes making the weirdest melodies.

But I stood mute in admiration. Of course I wouldn't have been a normal little child if I wouldn't have wanted to be tinkering with some of his instruments. My father most willingly showed me which hole to cover and where to blow. But then he proved not to be a good pedagogue. He expected that after one or two tries I would be able to produce the same result as he, whereas I could only bring forth hissing sounds. And right away I felt his disappointment.

And his impatience! It was always there. Although I could feel deep down how he loved me when he sometimes suddenly bent over and lifted me up and pressed me to his heart, patting my little head tight to his shoulder—oh, how good that felt—more often than not I felt his impetuous impatience. When I was walking around looking at the strange titles of his many books, he might pick out one, maybe in Arabic. Pronouncing a few words, he would have me repeat them. And if they didn't come out flawless, I saw his brow wrinkle; immediately I shrank back in fear.

Besides those highly treasured visits to his home, he in turn came to visit me in Kagran where my foster mother lived. He always brought some cookies and candies, which were most welcome. But woe was me if I saw another parcel in his hand! That usually did not mean that it could possibly be a toy; it usually meant some little tragedy. For instance, I remember so well how my father unwrapped such a parcel and said, "Now, Gusti, come and read this."

And never will I forget how he read for me to have me repeat: "Amos, amas, amat, amamus, amatis, amant."

And while the words meant "I love, you love, we love," they surely didn't mean that to me. They were saying loudly and clearly, "While I am a clever grown-up man, I have a moron for a daughter!" because, for some unknown reason, I didn't seem to catch on. Whatever he tried in his first Latin lesson of my life—I being eight years old—it didn't click with me. And all I could see was that impatient gesture and that disgusted expression on his face. And there was the man I wanted to please more than anybody else on earth! With a loud wail, I buried my face in his chest.

My father had several ways of making a little girl unhappy. Besides Latin and French grammar, there was his wish to break his daughter into traveling around the globe—beginning early. And so he conceived the awful idea of grabbing me from my foster mother's lap, putting me in a coat and hat, and more or less dragging me along with a satchel in my hand to some railroad station to show me some of the most interesting places in beautiful Austria. The only problem was, I couldn't care less.

Maybe it was because I had always lived so sheltered a life with such a small group of people that I was now so attached to them that even having to be away for more than half a day plunged me into deepest distress of homesickness. Being haunted by a most vivid imagination, I saw them in all kinds of peril and often in danger of death. Needless to say, it made me utterly unhappy. Such shyness existed between me and my father that I couldn't express my feelings in words.

23

I only, from time to time, quietly cried and then noisily blew my nose, which again made him roaringly impatient. There we were in Zell am See, looking toward the majestic glaciers. But instead of breaking out in appropriate oh's and ah's, I sobbed, "I am sure they are all sick back home."

I couldn't have displeased him more, and that happened every time we took a trip.

I remember one time when he wanted to show me the beauty and majesty of our great river, the Danube. We took the train up to a certain place where we stayed for a little while at an inn on the river where we watched the boats, freighters and cruisers go by. After a few days we would board such a cruiser and float down, passing all the historic sites where the Nibelungen had come and gone many hundreds of years ago.

When the boat finally landed at the big bridge, I looked up and, as is common on bridges, there were people coming and going in great numbers. With one shrill wail I cried out, "Here, they are coming from her funeral already." (I was sure my foster mother had died.) My humiliated father grabbed me and disappeared with me over the gangway into the crowd.

Again and again—I couldn't care less. Nibelungen, Danube, glaciers—all I wanted was my foster mother.

And then came the third big cloud on my childish horizon: my father insisted that I keep a diary. I was supposed to write down not only the happenings but also the impressions of every day. But all I could muster would be something like this: "I got up at 7 o'clock. I had to do my own hair. Had eggs for breakfast, which I didn't like. Had to visit a strange uncle, that I didn't like. And had to be quiet when Papa slept but had no book to read. I hope the day will soon be over."

Of course these kind of entries must not have been

very pleasant reading for my poor father. Somehow I sensed this, and I wanted to do better. In the hotel lobby I got hold of a guidebook through Bruck an der Mur, a town in Styria where we had just stayed in the hotel "Zum Goldenen Strauss." I grabbed the book, went to my room, and diligently copied: "Bruck an der Mur was founded by the Romans in the year so and so." And then I went down through its history. Then came another paragraph describing the surroundings.

I was very proud when I handed my diary over to my father that night. He took one glance, looked at the table where I had written, picked up the guidebook and threw it in my face. I was completely crushed.

From his insistence that I keep a diary, I surmise —and I'm sure that I'm right—that he must have kept a diary himself all his life. That would have been the most interesting reading matter for his daughter, but unfortunately I never saw his diary.

I can't help but feel sorry that my father didn't live until my teen years, because then he would have been delighted: I was an avid reader. I loved to play any kind of instrument, I was most interested in learning foreign languages, and my passion was "to go places," which at that time meant I was hiking crisscross through Austria with other young people. All of us belonged to the youth movement. Every summer we walked for weeks on end, crossing mountain passes and seeing the most remote vales and hills. Later my hiking instinct would go right into ship, railroad and airplane travel. I was the happiest when I was on the go.

But when I was nine years old, my father was found dead in his easy chair. He had slipped away during a nap.

That was the end of my childhood.

2

Learning to Hate

The most logical person to take over as my guardian after the death of my father, was the judge, to me Uncle Franz, who had married the oldest daughter of my foster mother. He was now living in our house.

He was a tall youngish man, always sitting, walking and keeping himself most erect. Later I learned that his colleagues called him a living paragraph sign—a very straight symbol—because he was such a stickler around the office.

The really most natural person to become my guardian would have been my brother, Karl. Much later I picked up little bits of information and learned that Karl was so upset about his long-lost father marrying again so shortly after he had discovered him that he was through with him entirely. He had no use for that new little sister either.

I never saw my brother until I bumped into him by chance in my graduation year. Then a very loose relationship developed. I visited him a couple of times in his bachelor quarters, and he gave me some books on nature. Then we lost track of each other again until after the war. An engineer colleague of his wrote to me in America that Karl had been bombed out but had been taken in by him and his wife. Immediately I began sending Karl packages regularly, which he always confirmed with a few heartfelt words of thanks.

In the fall of 1948 he wrote me a card: "What could I give my sister for Christmas?"

Since I had learned that he had strayed away from the church, I answered immediately, "What would make me most happy, dear Karl, is if you would go to the sacraments during midnight mass at Christmas Eve."

And this is what happened:

In December, 1948, I suddenly had a severe attack of kidney inflammation. This was on a concert tour, and I had to be left behind in St. Francis Hospital, Peoria, Illinois. Finally the family was informed that I was gravely ill with no human hope of recovery. On Christmas Eve I received the last sacrament of the church and, just before I fell into a coma, I offered my life for my brother's conversion.

Just around that time Karl had contracted a severe case of pneumonia and was placed in a hospital in Vienna. On Christmas Eve my big package had arrived, and he had just unpacked it on his bed: warm pajamas, a pair of fur slippers, fountain pen and pencils which he had asked for, and a camel's-hair bathrobe. And then the most delicious and unheard of delicatessens, which he fondled tenderly.

At that moment Cardinal Innitzer of Vienna made his Christmas rounds of the hospital and arrived at my brother's bed. The Cardinal told me later how my brother was sitting propped up with pillows, excitedly showing his precious presents.

Then he said, rather disheartened, to the cardinal, "All my sister wanted from me was that I go to midnight mass." And he added, "After fifty years."

When the nurse whispered to the cardinal that my brother was on the critical list, he said most kindly, "You know what? We'll give your sister her Christmas wish right here and now."

And he himself helped my brother to make a good confession and then gave him the last sacraments. When he said good-bye to him, my brother grabbed the new fountain pen and said with shiny eyes, "And now I am going to tell her."

He leaned his head back on the pillow and was gone.

When I awoke later out of my deep unconsciousness, coming back to life, I was handed a letter from Cardinal Innitzer, telling me of Karl.

* * *

After Father's death, fear entered my life. So far, like any other child, I had had my good times and my bad times. When I was disobedient, or when I broke things, or when I was careless or brought home bad marks from school, I was scolded dutifully by Mother and put into a corner. Or perhaps I was even punished as hard as having to go to bed without dinner when I had been just too fresh. But these short thunderstorms passed quickly, and then the sun would shine again from an undisturbed blue sky.

I had just entered the fifth year of school and was allowed to come and go by myself, not being chaperoned any longer by Kathy. I had greeted this with great glee because now we girls could fool around a little bit on the way to and from school, playing little games or chatting happily about this or that teacher, or telling each other what had happened at home, and finally stopping at the window of the grocery store or the bakery shop to look in at the treasures. But suddenly with one stroke this was stopped, and I wasn't allowed to mingle any longer with the others.

From now on it was different. Soon after Father's funeral, my Uncle Franz, my new guardian, made it clear to me that I had to come home from school non-stop, with no fooling around on the way. He said that he had his way of finding out everything, so I shouldn't try to hide anything or ever dare to lie to him.

From the beginning I tried to oblige him. Many a day when I came home my uncle stood in the doorway with a stick in hand, telling me he "knew all about it." Then he turned me over his knee and spanked me hard.

And when I remonstrated, "But, Uncle Franz, I came home right away! I didn't even stop a single time," he slapped me across the mouth and said, "Don't lie! I know everything."

This threat was hanging over me every day throughout those years. However desperately I might plead my innocence, nothing helped. My old foster mother cried bitter tears when she saw what was happening, and her daughter, my uncle's wife, joined her. She must have had a sad fate because I could hear her low crying behind closed doors almost daily.

Many years later, the poor man was taken to an insane asylum where he died, which explains everything. But at the time we didn't know that he was already sick. We only suffered under his cruel injustice, being punished for things we hadn't done.

So passed my eleventh and twelfth years.

Then a day came when suddenly it was as if someone had turned on a light switch in me, and I no longer had that dreadful fear of my uncle. All of a sudden I didn't care anymore what he might say or do, because I knew I would be beaten anyhow. I resolved, "All right. Why don't I do it all and at least be spanked for a purpose?"

And now all the things he had insinuated—that I was skipping school, playing hookey, hanging around with the other girls, asking him for money for copy books but instead spending it on cookies and candies —were put into action. Now an altogether new life began for me. Suddenly I blossomed. Thus far I had been a quiet, fearful child who hardly dared talk to people. Now I came out in the open—to the great astonishment of the girls in my class. I hooked elbows like we all used to do on the street, going in little groups of four or five abreast. I sang louder than the others. I laughed heartily at their jokes. I eagerly accepted an invitation to come upstairs in somebody's house, and I arrived home at any time—even after dark, stoically expecting my spanking—but having lived!

Something else happened at the same time when the switch was turned on. I suddenly felt a bottomless contempt for the man who had punished me all these years for no reason at all. Having lied to me by insinuating all these things which I had never done, I made up my mind that for this most cruel punishment I would never, as long as I lived, say one true word to him, so help me God. From then on a rather complicated process began. When Uncle Franz would ask me a harmless question, like "What did you have in school today?" and we had had arithmetic, history and needlework, as quick as a bunny I answered, "We had religion, German and physical education."

It absolutely had to be different from what was true.

At the mere word *religion* he usually burst into very abusive language. My uncle was a passionate adherent of the new socialist regime. In 1918 Austria had dismissed its emperor, who died afterward in exile, and taken on the government socialists, comparative only to the real Communists in Russia now, with no similarity to American socialists. One of the first actions

33

was to remove the crucifixes out of all schoolrooms and public offices. Their aim was to "enlighten" the general public about the true role of religion, namely, that it had been used by popes, bishops, priests and nuns to dull the minds of the people in order to make them more submissive to their rule. Usually they made up the spiciest stories about priests and nuns.

The new regime had not yet dared to outlaw religion as a subject to be taught in the schools, so we all attended religion classes. But all the other teachers and professors were of the socialist party, and they contradicted to the best of their ability whatever we had been told during religion class. All the Bible stories which I had loved so dearly in my childhood were now branded as silly old legends with not a word of truth.

This was the daily conversation during dinner. Involuntarily I lapped it up with a big spoon. It was different all right. Suddenly God was out of my life. But even at such an early age I felt an emptiness. How I envied my classmates for their warm friendship with God—while I was out in the cold.

How I went through high school successfully, I really don't understand, for I became accustomed to playing hooky and "enjoying life," which meant that I was already going for long hikes through the wheat fields and strips of woodland located next to the last houses of Kagran.

On these trips I was mostly alone, for only once in a while did I succeed in talking other girls into going along in my lawless life. I shudder now when I think what could have happened to me if I had gotten into bad company, because one step further and juvenile delinquency probably would have been my destiny. A whole flock of guardian angels must have watched over me.

I came back with armfuls of field flowers, poppies, bachelor's buttons and corn flowers, with which I unashamedly decorated our house, knowing they were a dead giveaway of my activities outside the classroom. But, thank God, I was a good student and somehow learned fast. Toward the end of each semester I led a very secluded life with my books, so I always "made it."

The Austrian report card used to have two words at its top. One word was *Betragen*, meaning behavior or conduct, and the second was *Fleiss*, meaning the degree of diligence the pupil showed in his work habits. After that came the twelve names of subjects for which he received grades. Unfortunately my impudence, my impetuousness, and my wrongly applied sense of humor constantly got me into trouble, so my first and second marks always caused an extra-hard spanking. But I deserved this. I was the horror and fright of my teachers. They couldn't possibly punish me enough; my imagination could always invent worse and juicier things of mischief. I remember how one teacher in my last school year, when I was fourteen years old, once called me out in front of the class, looked at me sternly, and said, "And I wish on you a daughter exactly like yourself. Sit down."

3

Learning to Live

When I was in Austria, a child spent five years in grade school followed by three years in high school. Then he had to decide whether he wanted to go on to higher learning or to learn a trade. In my last year of high school I felt an ever keener longing to go to the State Teachers' College of Progressive Education. The only trouble was that Uncle Franz could not see eye to eye with me.

"May I ask where the young lady is going to get the money for higher schooling?" he asked ironically.

I was too young and inexperienced to ever ask back, "Isn't there any money left from my father?" And I could have added, "And by the way, Uncle Franz, where are all his books? What happened to the birds? And where are all the instruments? And as long as we are at it, where are his diaries?"

Unfortunately these questions remained unasked, and to this day I feel bitterly sorry. Not so much for the birds, or the instruments or the books, although it would be interesting to see what he had collected during a lifetime, but his diaries certainly would have been the most interesting reading for me and probably would have been a key to his personality.

Well—just how does one get money for school? There was a girl in my class named Annie who lived about two hours away from Vienna in a famous resort section called Semmering. She told me that during the summer vacation she always earned "a lot of money" doing any number of little jobs in the fancy hotels there. One day she said, "Why don't you come and stay with us? I am sure it is all right with my mother."

Right then and there I made up my mind that I was going to spend the coming summer with Annie, making a lot of money in order to get into that school. But the first obstacle was, how would I ever get there? I was never given any pocket money, so I had nothing to save. And the railroad ticket would cost something.

School was over. I had graduated and done not badly at all. The first day of summer vacation had passed and the second one, and I got very itchy not to lose too much time. So on the third day I thought, *It's now or never!* I went up into the attic, looking for a receptacle in which to carry my belongings. The only thing I found was a huge straw suitcase the size of a footlocker. I put in my nightgown, a little underwear, a couple of dresses, my favorite books, and comb and toothbrush. All this rattled around in my big crate.

Then I waited until Uncle Franz took his nap after lunch. I knew he had the habit of emptying his pockets before he lay down. So I tiptoed in, grabbed all the money on his night table, anxiously watching that the clicking noise of the coins wouldn't wake him. Then I tiptoed out, grabbed my huge basket, kissed my old mother and Katie, and said "Auf Wiedersehn."

Once outside the house, I ran all the way to the trolley car. There I bought a ticket to the South Railroad Station. I still remember how apprehensive I was, watching anxiously whether just as the trolley took off, an infuriated Uncle Franz might show up. But, thank God, nothing happened. I was tense all the time as I walked up to the ticket counter and asked for a third-class ticket to Semmering, counting the coins and being terribly relieved that I had enough. The basket was too big to bring into the compartment, so I had to leave it on the train's platform. Therefore, throughout the two-hour trip I had to run back and forth, back and forth, watching that no one had taken it. It contained all my earthly possessions. Finally the conductor called out, "Semmering, Semmering."

I climbed down the steep steps of the train. Now I had to find out just exactly where Annie lived. I discovered it was quite a way. Many a time I rested and switched my big treasure from the left hand to the right hand and back to the left again.

Annie's father had died recently and her mother was earning her living as a laundress, barely making ends meet for herself and her seven children. But there was always room for one more, and she most graciously accepted me for the summer. Annie and I slept together on the floor while four little ones shared a big bed above us. I was so excited that first night that I hardly slept a wink. *Tomorrow, tomorrow,* I thought, *I am starting.*

So I did. I went from one hotel to the next. There were twenty-eight of them. First I offered my services as a "teacher" for children who might need help during vacation. My very appearance must have belied my grand title. I was as tall then as I am now, five feet seven and a half, and as thin as a beanstalk, with two long braids dangling down to my knees.

When I made the tour of the hotels the second time, I humbly and meekly investigated whether they needed anybody for anything. But those big men at the desk looked sternly and forbiddingly and shook their heads, and I came back close to tears.

Annie's mother consoled me and said that Rome wasn't built in one day either, and I shouldn't give up.

41

I had left "my address" in every place "just in case," and on the third day a page boy from the biggest hotel came running, summoning me to the manager. He asked whether I knew how to play tennis.

I answered cautiously, "Which rules do you use here?"

I simply hated to tell him that this was the first time I had heard the word and that I had no idea whether you played with your hands or your feet.

But the man seemed to take this as a very intelligent question. Evidently there were little differences, and he explained exactly what I had wanted to hear, namely, how they played the game. Then he told me that a tennis tournament was starting that very afternoon and the umpire had gotten sick. Would I pinch hit until they could find somebody else?

I most eagerly consented, and at one o'clock I climbed up to the tall seat. I spent the next week turning my head from left to right and right to left, calling out things I have now long forgotten. I don't know whether they couldn't find a better umpire or if they didn't try hard enough. Anyhow, they let me finish the whole week, and I was paid handsomely. On the last day on my high chair, I suddenly discovered that Uncle Franz was standing under some trees opposite me. Between following the ball, I made hissing sounds:

"If you don't leave immediately, I shall yell loud and tell everybody everything."

I really didn't know what I meant by that. I was just so upset about his very appearance. He moved over toward my seat and said soothingly that I had nothing to fear; he only wanted to know how I was, and that if I was all right he would leave. I only nodded, and that was it. This was the last time I saw him because I arranged all my visits to my old mother and to Kathy at times when I knew he would be at his office.

After my good beginning with the tennis people, I got several little jobs taking care of children until the end of the summer. By then Annie and I had both saved "a lot of money." At least it was enough to go in September to the State Teachers' College of Progressive Education for which both of us had passed the entrance examination. With the good results of the examination, plus the fact that I was an orphan, I was given a scholarship.

Before I entered the school, which was a boarding school, I sneaked up once more to see my old mother, told her everything I had done during the summer, and that I so very badly wanted to be a teacher. I still remember how I stopped suddenly because I almost said, "Would you pray for me?" when I discovered that I didn't believe that anymore. She took my face in her hands and kissed me tenderly and said it herself.

"There will never be a day, my dear child, when I won't take you to church with me and recommend you to God. I know all this will turn out all right."

One more kiss. One more grateful hug to Kathy who had had so much patience with me in my early years. And off I went to the new life.

4

Finally—The Truth

My scholarship provided for board, lodging and tuition, but everything else I had to earn. After World War I, the American Society of Friends, the Quakers, arranged a place in the Imperial Palace in Vienna where we could get embroidery work to do, for which we were paid by the inch. My friend from the mountain and I went there every other Saturday and got lingerie to embroider and received a check for the work we had done. The money I earned was needed for shoes, clothing, paper, schoolbooks, etc.

I never had money to pay for concert tickets, but I was hungry for music and in Vienna there was always music. On a Sunday morning I could just look in a newspaper and find that a mass by Mozart would be played in St. Stephen's Cathedral at 8 o'clock and a mass by Hayden in the Franciscan Church at 9 A.M.; then at 10:30 I would be running to be among the first in the Imperial Chapel at the Palace because the Vienna Philharmonic would play, the Vienna Boy's Choir would sing, and the bishop would celebrate the mass. The mass was uninteresting to me, but the combination of the choir boys and the philharmonic was the great weekly highlight which I almost never missed.

At this time I was passionately truthful because I had suffered so much in my childhood from untruth, and I didn't want to give the impression that I was attending the church service. I knew all about those priests and bishops, the pope, and what it all meant. I made sure that nobody mistook my presence in the church as an act of devotion, so I sat with my back to the altar on the steps of the side altar, deeply wrapped up in the music and making sure that nobody throught I was praying. So passed the four years in Vienna.

When I now think back on the four years in that school, it is with very mixed emotions indeed. First of all there was the school: State Teachers' College for Progressive Education, a brand-new creation of a very high academic standing in a country which was already famous for its excellent school system. But it was a monster. It tried to combine all the humanities of a preparatory school with the necessary extra-special courses for training teachers, such as psychology, methods, and pedagogy. Our professors were of the highest caliber. Some came from the university and, in fact, were much too good and a little too highbrow for us girls, but we certainly got a very thorough and wide education.

In spite of the social revolution, religion still existed as a subject also in this higher school. The poor young professor who instructed us was a theology professor from the university. He really suffered a "hell" in the true sense of the word. We were forced to attend his classes but we could at least make him miserable, and this we did. We came with the most outlandish doubts and really harassed him. And I was the worst.

Some of the girls were practicing Catholics, and there was even a chapel in our school building where a daily mass was held. Very soon I had my own gang of which I was the undisputed leader.

"Look at those Catholics," I used to say. "Isn't it ridiculous what they need to lead a decent life—seven sacraments, holy water, holy pictures, prayer books, Bibles, indulgences and whatnot. Well, we shall show them how we can get along without all those crutches, but we really have to be tops."

And so we tried to beat them in all subjects. For us, it was a matter of honor not to cheat, whereas we watched with scorn how "the holy water girls" got away with murder. Then they went to confession on Saturdays, and everything was fine again. We had only contempt for that.

Sad to say, my gang widened in membership. Finally we were the majority, trying to prove to ourselves and everybody else that a decent life can be lived without God and all those props.

On Palm Sunday of my graduating year I was aimlessly sauntering through the inner part of Vienna during the afternoon when I saw the people converge from all sides on the big Jesuit church. I thought, *Ah, Palm Sunday. It can only mean the St. Matthew Passion by Bach.* So I joined the group and was taken in with the stream of people into the very middle of the church. It was so densely packed that it was impossible even to faint. But there was no music.

It happened to be the last sermon in a series of lenten messages by the very famous Jesuit preacher, Father Kronseder. He talked about the crucifixion of our Lord Jesus Christ. Now I had heard from my uncle that all of these Bible stories were inventions and old legends, and that there wasn't a word of truth in them. But the way this man talked just swept me off my feet. I was completely overwhelmed by it, and I worked my way through the crowd to the pulpit. This was still in the old days when a sermon was given from a public pulpit. As he came down the stairs, I grabbed him by the elbow and said loudly and distinctly, "Do you believe all this?"

49

He took one look at me and took me by the arm and led me into the sacristy. He didn't want the dialogue heard in the church.

He looked at me and said, "Don't you?"

I simply said, "Of course not. I am from the State Teachers' College of Progressive Education." Our college was famous for being a socialist school.

He glanced at his wristwatch and said, "I'm very sorry. I have to be at the university in a quarter of an hour, but on Tuesday at four o'clock I'll have time and I will be waiting to see you. Good-bye."

Now here I was. I didn't want to be here on Tuesday at four o'clock because on Monday morning our whole class was going for the first time on a skiing vacation. Skiing had just started in the schools of Vienna, and I had put my whole heart into this trip which would take nine days. But now if I didn't show up on Tuesday at four o'clock, this man might think I didn't dare face him; and that was too much for me. I couldn't have lived with myself on that skiing expedition, so I let the others go and I got slowly but surely more and more worked up.

On Tuesday at four o'clock I was there in that church as this world-renowned professor came down the stairs and very kindly smiled at me, opened the door, and let me in. For two hours and ten minutes nonstop I threw at him all the accusations I had learned during my young life. He sat there in rapt attention and listened to me as if I had told him the most incredible scientific news. Then I was finished. He didn't say a word; he just looked at me.

Then I acted like a dripping faucet. One more thought came to my lips, then silence. He looked. Still another one, and another one, and then full silence. By then I felt as empty as a grain bag which had just been turned inside out and shaken.

He took a deep breath, leaned back, and said, "Well, my dear, you simply have been wrongly informed. That is merely a question of reading. I suggest you read this one book." And he scribbled down a title.

Then he looked at me and said, "You're Catholic, aren't you?"

I simply glared at him. Hadn't the man listened to me?

"If you have to fill out forms, what do you put down when it comes to religion?" he continued.

Dumbfounded, I had to admit that I would write down R.C. That was the way I was baptized, but I said, "But I have told you that it is all not true."

"Well, did you leave the church?" he asked.

"No, I didn't leave the church. I'm simply not in it."

"Well, if you haven't left the church then this is Easter time and you ought to go and do your Easter duties. When did you go to confession last?"

This was beyond me. I hadn't gone to confession.

"Well," he said, "then it really isn't very necessary that you add much."

He asked me a few leading questions and I meekly said yes or no. Then he looked at me so kindly, like I think our Lord must have looked at various people, and he said, "Take courage, I am going to pronouce the words 'thy sins are forgiven.' When I say these, God will simply eradicate your sins. He will forget them, and your soul will look like the soul of a newly baptized child."

At the moment when he said that, the sun suddenly hit the window behind him, and the sunlight formed a halo of light on his white hair. How that impressed my young romantic heart!

51

After he had said, "Ego Te Absolo," we got up and he shook my hand.

"Congratulations," he said. "Nothing can happen to you now. You are all right."

Then I found myself on the streets of Vienna, floating on a cloud and not looking where I was going. I walked right into an oncoming streetcar. The next thing I heard was voices. I was hit on the head, nothing bad, but I still remember that last feeling before I fainted: *Now I am going to die, and I am all right.* When it was ascertained that I had not been badly hurt, some kind person took me back to school in a taxi.

From the little bit the famous Jesuit Father had said to me, I realized that not only had I been wrong myself but I had been an instrument of the devil to get other people to go astray. Now I had only a few weeks left to make up for my error, because graduation was just around the corner. That turned me into a real missionary. I got the book the priest suggested and saw very factual, nonemotional, cold facts which were the absolute opposite of what I had learned from my uncle and schoolteachers. Now I walked around with this knowledge and tried desperately to regain all the lost souls I felt on my conscience. With the zeal of a crusader with fire and sword, half begging, half threatening, half buying, I got all but one. That one still hasn't believed.

As I look back on these solemn few hours, I know now what really happened in my soul. This priest was not only a famous theologian, a world-famous preacher sought after everywhere in German- and English-speaking countries, he also was a childlike, pious soul who really loved his Lord and Saviour. When I was finally finished throwing things at him, he looked at me with such true compassion and genuine love. He

52

made me understand how our Lord Jesus Christ had lived, died, and was crucified for me. Christ suffered His agony in Gethsemane and put up with all my aloofness and hardness of heart for only one reason —to win my love. He said it so simply and so convincingly that I was completely disarmed. And when he finally said, "Are you sorry now for what has happened?" I could truthfully say, with tears streaming down my face, "Yes, Father."

With this started a completely new life for me because now I was on the threshold of a new journey where Jesus, the heavenly Father, the Holy Spirit, and our grown-up sisters and brothers, "the saints" had suddenly turned from fiction to fact, from legend to reality, and my heart was eager to learn. Once again God was back in my life.

Graduation came and went. After graduation classes, some of the class made an excursion into the high Alps. We had a whole week of hiking a distance of between 2,000 and 3,000 meters (6,000 to 9,000 feet) across the ice fields and glaciers, enjoying the most unforgettable scenery, especially the sunset. One has to have experienced the sunset on a glacier to realize how deeply it impresses one's soul. Because I had had a little experience in mountain climbing, I was singled out by our guide to be the last one and to take the rope off and wind it up. So it happened that I was the last to stand there and watch the sinking sun turning to pink and red and casting shadows on the snow.

Suddenly I had to spread my arms wide and shout, "Thank You, God, for this great wonderful creation of Yours. What could I give You back for it?"

At that moment it crossed my mind that the greatest thing I could give to Him was this very thing I was so greatly enjoying. In other words, give up mountain climbing, give up hiking, give up living out in nature,

53

and bury myself in a convent which, to my recollection, was a dark place of medieval character.

With the generosity of my young heart I said, "Yes, Lord, here it is."

I walked straight down the slope and said good-bye to my colleagues. They stayed one more night; I couldn't wait, of course. I walked and ran all the way out of the valley to a small railroad train which eventually arrived in Salzburg the next morning at 6:30.

I still remember that as I arrived at the railroad station I saw a policeman standing there. I marched up to him and said, "Sir, could you please tell me which is the strictest convent in this town?"

He grinned at me and said, "I sure don't know. Ask this one," pointing to a Capuchin monk.

So I strolled over to the monk and again said, "Sir, can you tell me which is the strictest convent in this town?"

He looked at me slightly amused and said, "Yes, you go down to the Salzach River and follow it upstream to the fourth bridge. Cross that bridge and you will see a red onion tower halfway up the hill. That is the Benedictine Abbey of Nonnberg, and they are the strictest around here."

I said "Thank you" and found my way.

In less than an hour I rang the bell and asked to see the boss. I had to laugh now when I think back on those days, because I certainly didn't know the proper way in which to address the people. I didn't know that you said "Father" to a priest and "Reverend Mother" to a nun, and not "sir" and "boss."

I was ushered into a room and, to my great amazement, it was partitioned in half by a big grill. Rather amused, I marched up and down in front of it. Hanging on the other side were oil paintings of abbesses long gone.

I had to wait quite some time before the door opened and in came a small frail nun with a cross on her chest, a big ring on her slender finger, and the kindest eyes that have ever looked at me.

After searching for a moment, a very dear voice said, "What can I do for you, my child?"

Now here I was straight from the glaciers, brown as milk chocolate. Over my left shoulder I still had the coil of ropes. On my back I had a very heavy knapsack. In my right hand I had an ice pick with which I stood like Napoleon, pronouncing, "I have come to stay!"

The meek and mild voice inquired, 'Has somebody sent you, my child?"

I reared up to my five feet seven and a half inches and said, "Ha, if anybody had sent me, I wouldn't be here. I haven't obeyed anybody yet."

After these momentous words I was really and truly received into the Benedictine Abbey. The Reverend Mother must have had some other reason than the ones I gave her for taking me in. She never told me why I was admitted. As I look back on it now I cannot understand it because everything was set against it.

There at the abbey started two momentous years of my life.

5

On the Way

After Reverend Mother Abbess graciously had admitted me into the abbey, she found out—with eyebrows raised and an unbelieving look in her eyes—that she had admitted a tomboy. But it had been done, and the only thing to do now was to try to turn this creature into a girl before she could become a nun. Therefore, within two weeks I was given my private Mistress of Novices because I so very much did not fit the noviciate.

All I can remember of myself at this time was that I was, so to say, liquid goodwill. I so very much wanted to make good that I would have done anything and everything. But, in spite of that, I was constantly in trouble. First of all, one wasn't supposed to whistle. Well, I could understand why one shouldn't whistle worldly tunes, but what was wrong in whistling a hymn or Gregorian chant? It was hard for me to understand even though it was forbidden. Then one was supposed to take only one step at a time going upstairs and downstairs, whereas it was much quicker to come down the bannister, or two at a time. All these things had to be forbidden extra for me because Saint Benedict in the fifth century, when he wrote the famous Holy Rule, didn't think of mentioning these items. Therefore, I was not disobedient as yet.

I had been used to being outdoors as much as possible. Vienna has wonderful surroundings such as the famous Vienna Woods, and while at the boarding school we would spend practically every weekend on hikes and walks. The summers I spent in a youth group, we practically crisscrossed Austria on foot. So this was perhaps the most cutting sacrifice when I suddenly found myself in a cloistered community, surrounded by walls, a rather small garden sloping up a hill to the very foundations and buttresses of the famous Fortress of Salzburg—with very little possibility for me to get exercise.

Of course, I understood that all of this goes into the one big package deal with our Lord when I gave up His great wonderful creation and handed it back to Him. But I found out that there is a difference between the act of your free will on a mountaintop overlooking the glaciers and the daily executing of it, such as getting up at 5:00 A.M., getting dressed in deep silence, spending an hour and a half praying in Latin, and assisting at daily mass without uttering a word.

I would attend breakfast with my colleagues in deep silence, proceed to my work—whatever it was—in deep silence, while I was bursting at the seams to tell something or to ask something. But I had to wait until 1:00 P.M. when the bell rang and the deep silence was broken for one hour. But that didn't mean that I always had a chance to be heard, because that one hour was for all of us. Everyone wanted to get the ear of the Mistress of Novices. And whoever started talking first was heard first. Sometimes most of that precious hour was gone before it was my turn. At the signal of the bell, sometimes in the middle of a word, silence fell over us again. This was just one of my hardships.

It was absolutely unheard of that a humble postulant should contradict a superior nun. Now here I was from the State Teachers' College of Progressive Education in Vienna, thrown into the most medieval kind of little grade school still conducted in ancient rites. I was simply bubbling over with suggestions and contradictions. If it should happen that a postulant should contradict her superior, she had to kneel down and kiss the floor in repentance. I solved my situation this way: When I saw my immediate superior, the head mistress of the school, just come near me, I knelt down and kissed the floor. And then I said what I wanted to say. I couldn't understand that Saint Benedict would not agree to this.

Another hardship was that no one was supposed to make any remarks about the food. To my great astonishment, this was true even if one liked it—which wasn't always the case. One could not remark how good or bad the meal had been.

I remember at the beginning of lent in my beloved abbey that we in the noviciate were advised to write down our resolutions. In other words, what would we do as an extra act to show our love for God? Some would say they would skip a meal a day. Another might vow to get up half an hour earlier for more prayers. I still remember my little script which said, "I will not whistle. I will not come down any bannister. I will not go up on the roof and jump over the chimney. laugh out loud in a time of deep silence and so on."

Dear Reverend Mother Abbess added in red ink: "Good for you, Maria." I still have this precious document somewhere among my belongings.

I don't know why it happened that I constantly broke something—a cup, a saucer, a penholder. There was a rather humiliating penalty for this. The culprit had to bring the broken object with her and, before the next meal with the whole community assembled, she had to kneel down and pronounce, "I, the most unworthy member of this holy community, have wasted common good."

Next she had to hold up high what she had broken. Then she had to lie down flat on the floor, and the meal began. The first time Mother Abbess would let her lie there during the soup course, and then a gentle knock on the table would indicate that she could get the second course. But as I appeared more and more times, I had already made it only to the dessert.

Once some little evil spirit got into me after I had broken a big ceramic plate. I pasted it together at the break and then carefully knocked out the inside, leaving only the rim. And when I knelt down, I held the whole thing like a window for my face to look through and pronounced, "I, the most unworthy member of this holy community, have wasted common good," lifting up my halo.

Then I lay down through soup, through the main dish, through the salad and through the dessert. The whole community had left and I was still lying there, very much troubled and worried that they had forgotten me. After a little while I heard a knock and there were just two of us, Reverend Mother and myself.

She asked me very gently, "Will that be the last time now, Maria?"

And I promised what I had no right to promise because it wasn't the last time. But I frantically tried to be more careful.

As I look back on those years, I realize now that they were the first times in my life that I was really disciplined. The beatings of my uncle didn't count. That was not discipline.

In the boarding school there were certain rules and regulations I had to keep, but if one kept within the boundary nothing much could happen. Although I was never on the honor list for good behavior, there was not much punishment. These months—these two years —were really necessary to get my twisted character and my overgrown self-will cut down to size. I learned merely by daily observance to curb my self-will, to keep my mouth shut when I was almost bursting at the seams, to obey even if I didn't understand why—and, thank God, all of this for the love of Him who, as Father Kronsader had said, "had died for me." As it used to be said in the Catholic wedding ceremony, sacrifice is usually irksome, but love can make it easy, and perfect love can make it a joy.

But as I look back on those two precious years I have to add hastily that they were by no means all hardships and trouble. I had never known a real warmth of homelife. Our noviciate was the first place where I really felt at home, secure and loved. Our Mistress of Novices (after a few months I was taken in with the others) understood beautifully how to make us love each other in word, in song, in deed. She showed that we cannot love God whom we do not see if we do not love our neighbor whom we do see—even if our neighbor had a terrible habit of clicking her rosary all the time, or if she got on your nerves by saying, "But, but," and looking reproachfully at you most of the time.

Now it had turned into my very own home, and the fifth graders, my own class, were like my very own children.

In looking back at this time I simply have to laugh loud and long when I see how I, from the "State Teachers' College of Progressive Education," was grafted on this old plant, the little school at Nonnberg, where everything was done in the old-fashioned way. I had learned to push the school benches back against the wall, sit with my children on the ground, having clay for them, and colored paper, and start every day with handicraft and not with the pages of some bone-dry grammar, and put as much as I could into music.

After all, I was privileged to be among the first to witness progressive education. Our college was the very mother house, the very cradle from where it went all over the world. How well I remember that during our practicing period when we were launched on teaching little children under supervision, we always saw strangers sitting in the rear. They came from a place called Columbia University in New York City. And now here I was in old Nonnberg.

My class loved me dearly. Between September and Christmas we had already learned forty-seven songs by heart. It was always one of my strong points to tell stories, and so my classes in geography and history and in the German language—the equivalent of English classes in this country—were the most lively taught. I was a little bit horrified when around Christmas I realized that I had forgotten completely to teach grammar and arithmetic. But I simply got my children together and told them. I confessed that we had to work overtime now to make up for lost time. They were such good sports; they really rattled down the multiplication tables. In an incredibly short time, we had the subject and predicate, object, third clause and fourth clause under control, and my conscience eased up again because now the great day that threatened was just around the corner.

The superintendent of schools would pay his yearly visit to Nonnberg and sit in on every class. By the grapevine I had heard that he had a hobby of tracing everything back to the sun. He would ask the children what makes the railroads go, and it was not the steam and it was not the engine. Ultimately it was the sun. And so I impressed this on my class. Every thinkable object I had traced back to the sun.

We have a very famous epic in German: *The Nibe-lungenlied*. I divided it into as many parts as I had children, giving each the same size of blue wrapping paper. I had colored sheets of paper in the middle of the floor, and each had to reproduce whatever scene I assigned to them. We put it together in one long pano-rama around the wall. On another day I took one tall sunflower and put it in a flowerpot in the middle of the floor. Every child was given a long narrow sheet of paper on which he had to paste paper petals and stems torn from yellow and green paper. These made about forty-five beautiful sunflowers which were the decora-tions of our classroom.

When the great day came and the feared sovereign school superintendent entered our room, his eyes fell on the sunflowers and he smiled. We greeted him with a song sung in parts that made him smile a little more. And then he slowly but surely asked, "Children, have you ever seen a trolley car in Salzburg? Now, I won-der, what makes the trolley car go?"

And to his great delight, the whole class shouted, "The sun!"

Well, I was way ahead on the line. Afterward at a conference of all the teachers with him, I was set forth as an example and cited as an excellent instructor. And every one of the venerable old nuns was sup-posed to ask my advice on how to turn the Nonnberg Grade School into a Progressive School in Salzburg. He congratulated Reverend Mother for having me!

How very understanding my superiors were that they chose me to take the various classes on their yearly May outings. Starting with the first grade, which just went around the town, I took the second grade, which went a little farther up to Hellbrun where there was a little zoo; the third grade which went all the way up the Gaisberg, the mountain behind the town; and finally the last grade, mine, the fifth grade, which was allowed to stay overnight near a famous waterfall. That made us all happy—the parents, the children and, last but not least, me.

And so the months passed and the first year was gone, and Mother Abbess had a little more hope that I would pass the final test of being taken from the status of candidate into the status of novice when again I discovered that God's ways are not our ways, and His thoughts are not our thoughts.

6

For "Ten Months Only"

One day I was sitting in the candidate's living room correcting papers of my fifth graders when somebody tapped me on the shoulder. I looked up and there was old Sister Lucia beckoning me to come outside. There she whispered, "Reverend Mother wants to see you."

Before I could close my mouth, which had opened wide in astonishment, Sister Lucia had already disappeared because it was not customary for the lay sisters to have conversation with the candidates. And so I couldn't ask the burning question, "Why?" There was nothing I could do but follow the summons. Reverend Mother's parlor happened to be on the extreme other side of the ancient abbey, which gave me a little time to wind my way slowly down the stairs and across the cobblestone kitchen yard, thinking hard all the time, *Just what does she know?*

It was so unheard of for a candidate to be called into Reverend Mother's private parlor, because all the disciplinary and other business was done by the Mistress of Novices. I got the painful feeling that it must be something real big. Searching my conscience, I couldn't imagine anything so tremendous. Even in this perplexing situation I took in some of the great beauty of our old abbey. Fourteen hundred years had contributed to make it what it was: the most beautiful convent north of the Alps—Romanesque traces of the church walls, the Gothic choir which I could see through the window. Down through the Baroque period until that very moment the beautiful red onion tower of the church had cast its shadow on the courtyard. I reached the herb garden, which I knew quite well, and as usual the place emanated its own peace and tranquility.

Then I had reached the door to Reverend Mother's room. The walls were so thick and the door so heavy that I hardly heard upon my shy knock her friendly "Ave," which is the Benedictine equivalent to our modern "Come in." I stopped right inside the door, looking anxiously at Reverend Mother's face, which after one moment of scrutiny did not seem overly clouded or upset.

"Come here, my child," she said in a friendly manner. "Sit down. Tell me, Maria, I want to know how much you have learned here. What is the most important thing in life?"

I couldn't suppress my deep sigh of relief. Was that all she wanted to know? This I had really learned. So I said most joyfully and most convincingly, "The most important thing in life is to find out what is the will of God and then to go and do it."

Reverend Mother looked at me for a moment and then asked, "Even if it is hard?"

I simply shrugged my shoulders. "Of course, even if it is hard."

"All right, Maria," she said. "There was a certain Baron Georg von Trapp who was here today to see me. His wife died some years ago and he is now left with his seven motherless children. One child has barely recovered from a severe attack of scarlet fever and now has a murmur in her heart. Therefore, the doctors and teachers advised him to take her out of school for one year and have her tutored at home. It seems to be the will of God that you are the one we can spare and send out to teach little Maria."

"Sent out—sent away? Reverend Mother!" I exclaimed, horrified, "I want to stay *here!* I don't want to go away!"

"Even if it is the will of God?" she simply asked.

Then I had to eat my own words.

She went on: "Baron von Trapp was a captain in the Austrian Navy, one of the great heroes of our nation."

"Captain?" I interrupted her.

My horror grew. I was a girl from the mountains. I had never seen the sea. The only way I had come in contact with a sea captain was through the silent film version of *Mutiny on the Bounty.* And now she wanted to send me to a *captain!*

The Reverend Mother tried her utmost to put me at ease, explaining what a kind person he had seemed to her and that I would only be loaned for ten months.

"In ten months you will return to the convent to stay—for good."

That sounded a little better, but only a tiny little bit. In between the "for good" lay ten months of being away in the house of a captain.

In our abbey it was the custom that when we entered, our worldly clothes were given to the poor. Only the clothes from the last candidate to enter were kept in case somebody had to leave again. The last candidate's outfit was quite a sight. A brown gown that we would call a midi today, with latticework around the neck and the sleeves, high black shoes with laces, and a leather hat looking like a fireman's helmet.

When I finished dressing, the Mistress of Novices exclaimed, "How very elegant. Oh, how pretty."

Well, she hadn't been out in fifty-two years, so I

suppose I must have looked to her like I was wearing the latest fashions.

I took my guitar and a satchel with my few belongings, then consisting of underwear and books—the brown dress being my only one—and I knelt down for a tearful farewell when Reverend Mother made a sign of the cross on my forehead and wished me God's choicest blessings. I wasn't even given time to round up my colleague candidates, who were doing different chores at the time, to say good-bye.

With my eyes full of tears, I stumbled over the century-old threshold and walked down the 144 steps from old Nonnberg into Salzburg. I was told to go to the bus station and take the bus marked Aigen. The bus driver attracted my attention because he could talk while balancing a toothpick between his teeth. I asked him where I had to get off and how I would find the big mansion of Baron von Trapp. He explained to me just how to reach the mansion. With tear-stained cheeks, I walked the long way around a big garden until I came to the gate and rang the bell. After a few moments a distinguished gentleman wearing white gloves opened the gate.

I didn't know how to greet a captain, so I made a curtsy and said, "How do you do, Captain," and extended my hand to shake hands.

The butler, however, knew better. I never got to a handshake. He bowed a little stiffly and showed me into the living room.

There I stood—my God and I—on a new threshold of life. I had come from the middle ages in the convent into the beautiful and most elegant home of a baron.

7

Baroness von Trapp

And now—to make a long story short—I fell in love! For the first time in my life. I fell in love with those wonderful children. There they were—from age four to fourteen—two boys* and five girls. I don't know exactly how it happened, but in no time we were just one heart and one soul.

The captain was not at home when I arrived. There was the most dignified elderly lady, Baroness Matilda, who kept house for him and who had introduced the children to me—especially young Maria who was to be my pupil.

Now a completely new life started to unfold. For the first time in my life somebody took me around the neck and hugged and kissed me. As I looked back now, it really *was* the first time. In my old foster mother's house there wasn't any hugging and kissing done. Of course, under the grim regime of my guardian there wasn't any tenderness anywhere. And strange enough, neither was there any of it in the boarding school. I had many good friends, but we were just good sports and I simply don't remember having ever kissed anybody.

That makes me realize what harmless and innocent young girls we had been. This was fifty years ago, with no radio or television around. No illustrated papers were throwing sex at us. The men in our lives were our professors, mostly elderly gentlemen. Some of our "love stories" had to do with young and pretty lady professors whom we venerated in the dust and imitated minutely. I still remember how I once got hold of a water glass from which my idol had drunk and which I kept in my night table to take a sip from every morning. With careful rationing I stretched it over two weeks.

Even on our long hikes with the youth group, where we were twenty girls and twenty-four boys—I don't really remember any special love stories. The boys usually walked and climbed ahead and, when we girls arrived, arrangements for the night were made and the water in the kettle was boiling already. When I think of these happy times I feel bitterly sorry for our young people today who cannot enjoy such undisturbed happy times.

And then I was at Nonnberg where kissing was restricted to Reverend Mother's ring.

Now here I was, sitting on the carpet in front of the fireplace with a roaring fire going, telling stories to the little ones when suddenly Martina crawled on my lap, hugged me tight, and covered my face with kisses. I was almost petrified. But then the ice was broken, and I opened my arms wide and held them all at once as tight as I could.

And that is my own true real love story.

As the months passed, the captain came and went and I came to like him quite well because he joined in our games, went bicycling with us, or hiking up the mountains behind the house, or sat with us in front of the fire playing the violin while I played the guitar and all of us sang. But that was all it was: a very good time.

In fact, I was quite elated when Baroness Matilda told me one day that there was a good chance that the baron was going to marry again. There was a Princess Yvonne, a distant cousin of his first wife.

"Oh, that's wonderful!" I exclaimed. "Then the children will get a mother again."

Again God had ordained it otherwise, and what I would never, never have imagined happened. There came the day when Baron Georg von Trapp asked me to stay with him and become the second mother to his children.

God must have made him word it that way because if he had only asked me to marry him I might not have said yes, because at that time I really and truly was not in love. I liked him but didn't love him. However, I loved the children, and so in a way I really married the children.

Now I had it all figured out for myself: Of course I was only loaned from Nonnberg. Reverend Mother had said ten months. If I had to marry in between, it would take a little longer, I rationalized, until little Martina, age four, would be able to take care of herself, or the older sisters and brothers might perhaps take over. And then, of course, there wasn't any question of having children. I was only to bring up those which he already had. This was some forty years ago when there was next to no sex education. I had, of course, studied in college how babies came about and are eventually born. But I made one fatal mistake: I thought *it* only happens if you want children. That's why I congratulated myself and, as far as I was concerned, I wasn't really leaving Nonnberg completely, I was only extending my leave of absence.

I was so convinced about all of this that, the night before our wedding, I still said to the captain, "Georg, I still think it wouldn't be quite necessary to get married only in order to bring up your children."

I still remember how he looked at me so very lov-

77

ingly and put his hand on mine and squeezed it a little bit. That was his answer—except I didn't understand it.

When I did understand it—it was too late. Then I was in a terrific inner turmoil. I felt betrayed—betrayed by the One to whom I had vowed my life and my future, whose will I was eager to do, and of whose faithfulness I was so sure. Now He had lured me into this situation and shown me clearly that His feelings for me were not the same as mine for Him.

This is the way Jacob must have felt when after seven years of faithful serving, he married—or so he thought—his beloved Rachel. A Jewish bride at that time was, however, heavily veiled. When Jacob awoke the next morning he found at his side Leah, Rachel's older and ugly sister!

Christ had given me, His bride, to the baron! I was furious and I had to tell Him so the very next day. I had asked my new husband to postpone our honeymoon because one of the boys, Werner, had a high fever and I wouldn't have felt comfortable away from the children. I had even suggested that he go ahead on our honeymoon, which he politely declined, telling me we could go later. Around noon I stalked into our little parish church, right up front to the communion rail. I did not make a genuflection, with which we Catholics acknowledge the true presence of God in the Eucharist kept in the tabernacle.

I stood there, stiff and blazing mad, and said, "If any human man had done this to his bride—namely, arranged for her to marry another man while she thought he was as much in love with her as she was with him—I wouldn't think much of him. You have done just that! And You knew that I only wanted *You*. All right. You didn't want me. Now I don't want You anymore." I turned around and stalked out.

It happened to be the beginning of the time of Advent, the preparation for Christmas. I didn't want to go to church, so on the first Sunday I developed a terrific headache. On the second Sunday I was writhing in bed with sudden stomach cramps. And so I mysteriously fell sick every Saturday night in order to be quite well again for the beginning of the next week, when I suddenly discovered something. For a few nights in a row I noticed that the little ones, after our official night prayer was over, did not rise from their knees but covered their little faces with their hands and prayed on for a little while most fervently. Finally I learned that they were asking God to make their mother well enough so she could go to midnight mass with them.

I didn't want to disappoint them. So we went together to our parish church a little ahead of time in order to stand outside with all the other people and listen to the Christmas carols being played on trumpets from the steeple and watch as many "glowworms"—people from the mountain farms carrying lanterns as they came to midnight mass—descended from the mountains. It was a beautiful sight and a wonderful introduction to the Christmas spirit. As I went into the church with the little ones holding hands, I looked straight forward and said to God, "I'm only here because I didn't want to disappoint the children. I didn't come because of You." I was still so hurt and wanted to make sure that the Lord knew how I felt.

Next the little ones tugged on my sleeve and wanted to see the Christmas crib. The whole altar in the side chapel had been turned into the town of Bethlehem, and there were the figures of Mary and Joseph and the little infant in the manger, almost life-size. As we stood and looked, a strange thing happened. While you can quarrel with a grownup, how can you quarrel

79

with a newborn baby who has stretched out his little arms for you to pick him up?

And so God in His eternal mercy and love had gotten around my stubborn heart once again and had come with all the love which prompted Him to come into the cold cave outside Bethlehem. I placed the children in a pew and asked them to keep my seat while I went to confession and got rid of all my hurt and hard feelings. Once again God came back into my life.

From that Christmas on, life was altogether different. I understood more and better my husband's love, and by and by I learned to love him more than I have ever loved before or after. For the rest of all our years together we always celebrated our wedding anniversary on Christmas Day.

The second marriage when the first marriage was not happy must be a great thing. You can do all the things your poor husband had been deprived of, and you can really glory in being bigger and better every day of your life. However, if the first marriage has been a very happy one, then it is not that easy. Somehow I felt that. So one day after I was married for a few months, I said, "Georg, how can I make you happiest?"

He looked at me with his good, beautiful dark eyes and said, "By being exactly like Agatha." That was the name of his first wife.

I wanted to surprise him. So, fortified with pencils and pad, I made the rounds of those cousins who had been her best friends and near to her same age. I went from one castle to another and finally ended up in Vienna, where her sister was living, all the while filling my note book with the answers to my stereotype question: "What was Agatha like?"

"Well—she was very quiet. Very kind. She loved to

knit. She did not like to hike or other sports. She loved having babies, and so she always was either expecting one or nursing one." That was the main outcome of my research.

I was blown up with good intentions. While I was pretty much convinced that Agatha and I were like night and day and it would be hard to find two women who were more opposite, there was no question in my mind that I could bridge the gap and simply *become like Agatha.* Even as other people want to learn as grownups to play an instrument and therefore dedicate hours and hours to practicing on the cello, the violin or the piano, I devoted my time to my project: to become like Agatha.

First I bought knitting needles and wool, went back to Nonnberg, and found a nun who could show me how to knit. Sadly enough, I had never learned. Having decided to knit socks for my new husband, I found myself a comfortable easy chair in which to sit from then on and to act like Agatha.

I must have knitted about five inches' worth of stocking when Georg came into my room, stared at me, and said, "What are you doing there?"

Meekly I answered, "I am knitting, Georg, like Agatha."

He shook his head and said, "Let's go bicycling."

That disturbed my program.

"But, Georg," I said, "Agatha did not go bicycling with you. Please sit down with me and let's talk."

He shook his head, got himself a chair, sat down and looked me over. He couldn't quite understand what was going on. I stared at my knitting because every time I glanced away, I dropped a stitch and frowningly had to regain it.

I was waiting. I had heard that Georg used to sit

with Agatha by the hour and tell her stories from the navy. Why didn't he start?

Georg still looked unbelievingly at my handiwork and said laughingly, "When do you think those stockings will be finished?"

Now I was hurt. Of course I didn't knit very fast yet. In fact, I could hardly knit at all. But he didn't see my goodwill.

So I stubbornly kept on knitting and knitting and waiting and sitting in my chair for Georg to see my great love, because wasn't I slowly becoming exactly like Agatha?

This lasted about ten days. Then Georg came into my room again, got his chair very close to mine until our knees touched, put his hands on mine so I couldn't continue knitting, and said, "Now tell me, what is bothering you? We're not going for hikes anymore. We're not playing volleyball, we're not making music together, not bicycling anymore—WHY?"

By then tears came streaming down my cheeks and I cried aloud, "Because I want to become like Agatha!"

Georg took my knitting and threw it in the corner. He pulled me out of my chair and held me tight, and said, "I didn't mean it that way. If you are as kind as she, that is good enough for me. Otherwise, please be yourself."

And that was the end of that. From that moment on I was really in love. The real me—Maria—with my Georg.*

* The details that follow this time in the author's life may be found in her book, Story of the Trapp Singers (Philadelphia: Lippincott, 1949).

8

The Third Reich

"And they lived happily ever after," one could almost say as the years went by.

We had two hobbies in our family. One was to hike together and the other was to sing together. Both would prove very important one day for the Trapp family.

The people were used to seeing us come out of our house dressed for mountain climbing with big knapsacks on our backs and mountain boots, walking around our garden fence to the little station where the local trains stopped that took us into the Alps.

The people were also used to hearing us sing together by the hour on summer evenings. Sometimes we could sing those many beautiful Austrian folksongs nonstop for two hours without repeating.

On our estate we had a chapel, and one day the bishop sent a new priest to say mass for us. That was the turning point in our life because Father Wasner was a musical genius. When he heard us sing he was quite enthusiastic that there should be a choir made up of our whole family. In the meantime Werner had turned into a tenor and Rupert into a bass.

Father Wasner acquainted us with the glory of the a cappella music of the sixteenth, seventeenth and eighteenth centuries. For the sheer joy of singing we continued sometimes for four or five hours. The word

85

amateur comes from the Latin *amare*, "to love." We started out as true amateurs; but having such a great musician as our director, we slowly turned into professionals without knowing it. We were truly "discovered" by the great opera singer, Lotte Lehman, who heard us behind the screen of hemlock trees in our park and, through her persuasion, finally got my husband's permission for us to give a concert during the Salzburg Festival. He shuddered at the mere thought of having his family on stage. Being an Imperial Navy officer and a member of the aristocracy, that just wasn't done. But Lotte Lehman, a great artist and a great lady, finally convinced him there was nothing undignified in it, so "just for this one time" he allowed it. A new chapter in our lives began that very same day.

During the festival, managers from all over the globe assembled in Salzburg. After this one performance we were offered contracts from every country outside the Iron Curtain, even from the United States. The captain bought a scrapbook and we pasted these contracts in as souvenirs. Little did we know that this very scrapbook would be our most precious possession, in fact our life line, in the black days ahead.

Salzburg lies on the very edge of Austria, only a few miles from the German border. But we were such homebodies that we only heard the distant thunderlike noise that was going on across the border—how Hitler had taken over the government, how he was giving more and more daring speeches—but it all seemed so far away and so unreal. The one great hardship which befell us was the bankruptcy of the bank where my husband had invested the family fortune. The bank had failed after Hitler had closed the border, not allowing any Germans to cross over into Austria. Since Austria depended almost entirely on the tourist trade, two consecutive years with no tourist was the downfall of many people and eventually the bank. We were not as hard hit as many others because we still had our big estate and many precious objects of art and a little money.

Then it happened. We were all sitting in our library listening to the voice of Chancellor Schuschnigg bidding farewell to Austria which was giving way to force. The very next thing was the German anthem and the tremendous roar of "Heil Hitler!" It was the night of the 12th to 13th of March, 1938, a date we shall never forget. Austria was wiped off the map and incorporated into the "Third Reich."

The door of the library opened and our butler came in, went over to my husband, and said, "Captain, I have been an illegal member of the party for several years," and he showed us his swastika.

This was all so overpowering and so overwhelming that it left one numb.

The very next day going into town—what a change. From every house hung a swastika flag. People on the street greeted each other with outstretched right arm, "Heil Hitler!" and one felt absolutely like one was in a foreign country

At first we waited for the storm to blow over. My husband did not allow the swastika around the house or the new greeting or the new anthem to ever be heard. The pressure mounted and our lives were threatened by the Nazis.

So half a year passed, and then came the moment when my husband called the family together and said, "Now we have to find out what is the will of God. Do we want to keep our material goods, our house, our estate, our friends—or do we want to keep our spiritual goods, our faith and honor? We cannot have both any longer."

Then he looked at his children and said, "Listen, you can have money today and lose it tomorrow. The very same day you can start all over again, and that can happen more than once to you in your lifetime. But once you have lost your honor or your faith, then you are lost."

There was no real question what God wanted. As a family it was decided that we wanted to keep *Him*. We understood that this meant we had to get out.

9

Trapp Family Singers

It is absolutely incredible how silly and careless I had been when I packed my rucksack. In order to get away inconspicuously we had to pretend to do what we had done so many times before—go on a hiking trip in the mountains. When I started to unpack my rucksack on the other side of the Alps in that tiny Italian village, I found five voluminous petticoats that went with my feast-day national costume.

The content's of my children's rucksacks weren't much better. I found ski boots which we really didn't need in New York later, and even one beloved teddy bear named Timmy.

What was I thinking of when I took all those petticoats? All I can say is, "I don't know!"

The bottom had dropped out of my world. Austria was gone. All the plans we had made for the future of our children had been scrapped. So what does it matter what one grabs to put in the rucksack? Everything seems so unimportant when one's country is no more.

In my husband's rucksack, however—thanks be to God!—was the scrapbook with all the valuable contracts. Besides this there was also the flag from his submarine with the red and white colors of Austria.

Overnight we had become really poor; we had become refugees. A refugee not only has no country, he also has no rights. He is a displaced person. At times he feels like a parcel which has been mailed and is moved from place to place.

The first burning question for us was: "How do we keep going?" After all, there were two parents and nine and a half children—yes, the tenth was on the way. The only thing we could do well together was sing, so we had to turn a hobby into a way of making a living.

In the beginning we sang for just anything—a birthday party, a wedding, a devotion in church—until answers came back from the managers we had written, the men whose contracts were pasted in our scrapbook.

Soon things began to happen. We were invited to sing in Milan which, we learned afterward, is the gateway to the music world of Italy. As this concert was most enthusiastically received, other engagements followed in Turin, Florence and finally Rome. We were such a novelty in the music world—a choir composed only of members of one family—that we drew everybody's attention until we were received by Mussolini and afterward at court in Rome. We also attended an audience with the Holy Father, Pious XI, and sang for him the "Ave Verum" by Mozart.

Then real tragedy struck. People began to talk, pointing at us, saying, "This Trapp family! They are not Jewish! They didn't have to leave Austria. Just *why* did they leave?"

To our untold horror, we noticed that people began to distrust us because they thought we might be spies for Hitler. Nobody seemed to be able to believe that one would voluntarily leave everything behind only and solely for one's conviction. And, sure enough, Italy told us to get out.

Since we couldn't go back home, we had to go on. And so it happened all over Europe—from Italy we went to France and began singing again at the bottom, making our way up to a big gala concert in Paris, when again we were asked to leave. No country wanted us for more than a couple of months at the most. So we went from France to Belgium, to Holland, to Denmark, to Sweden and to Norway, always singing and saving every penny for the last contract in our precious scrapbook: the USA. And we finally made it.

In Oslo, Norway, we boarded a ship which must have been a first cousin of Noah's ark. We went down to its very belly, where we were surrounded by fellow refugees. But the main thing was, the ship was heading for New York. It took twenty-two days to get there, but finally we passed the Statue of Liberty and went ashore. My husband could barely stop me from kneeling down and kissing the ground of America, the promised land.

In the moment of great joy in having arrived in the USA, I got us all into trouble. As I came to the immigration officer, he asked the usual question, "How long do you intend to stay in the United States?" Instead of saying "Three months," as our visitor's visa read, I blurted out, "I hope forever." That was bad. Immediately it put us with the "suspects" who were marched off to Ellis Island where we spent three days and three nights, full of anxiety. The place was crawling with rumors. There was a group of Chinese people there who had already crossed the ocean three times because the United States refused to accept them. The shipping line was then compelled to take them back to the other side. That meant that we might have to go back into the bowels of our ancient ship and stay on it for the duration of the war because we couldn't go back to Europe and we had no visa for any country. If America would not accept us, we would spend the next years "in the belly of a whale." What a future!

But after three days of being examined and interviewed, the authorities must have finally realized we were not spies because we were released.

This was the rather dramatic beginning of the Trapp Family Singers. We have a proverb in German: "Aller Anfang is schwer," which means: "Every new beginning is hard." This was very true, for the next months were hard in America.

In looking back, it is hilarious what mistakes we made in everyday English. But as we had arrived with only four dollars in cash between us, there was no question of ever taking English lessons. We learned the hard way by making mistakes and pointing at things and finding the words.

Our two older children, Agatha and Rupert, knew English quite well from school and from spending a few months with their English relatives in London. Also, my husband's English was quite good. The rest of us depended on them as our teachers.

These times I have explained in detail in my first book, *Story of the Trapp Family Singers*. I also told how our bishop in Salzburg advised Father Wasner to go with us. Since he had been the publisher of a Catholic weekly paper and the only one who was unrelentingly anti-Hitler, the bishop felt that his days outside the concentration camp could be counted. Father Wasner is a natural linguist; languages simply jump at him. I remember when we were in Sweden he bought a newspaper at the railroad station and told us what was in it, never having seen a Swedish word before. The same thing happened in all the other countries, and we used to exclaim, "But, Father, how in the world can you understand what you are reading?"

He would say, "Well, after all, I have had eight years of Greek, eight years of Latin, and six years of Hebrew." So, for him, English was a cinch.

I remember how I often made people laugh out loud when I said something which was meant to be very solemn, for instance, "As it says, the ghost is willing but the meat is soft."

Another daily problem was the complete lack of money. Each of us was allotted twenty-five cents for breakfast, thirty-five cents for lunch, and fifty cents for dinner. I still remember vividly how the Trapp family came into the dining room of a hotel in Alfred, New York, where we were to sing at the university. We had already sat down and the waitress was distributing the menus, but, horrors, the cheapest dinner was one dollar. Whereupon the whole Trapp family got up and walked out in search of the nearest diner where we could eat for fifty cents.

Not the least of my personal problems was how I could possibly conceal that our tenth baby was on the way. Thank God, back home I had a very shrewd little seamstress. When I had told her my misgivings, she said consolingly, "Oh, there's really nothing to it. All you have to do is make sure you are always a little fuller above than below."

"But, Mimi," I said helplessly, "how in the world can I do that? I know me; I always get enormous."

"Let me do it for you," Mimi said. And then she went to town and bought three different sizes of dresses and did something to them. When she handed them to me finally, she said, "Now, listen. Every morning you step in front of a tall mirror and hold a book, and when it is flush, take the next size."

And this is exactly what I did—and it worked!

There are two kinds of people who always know tomorrow's news today: managers and newspaper people. Three weeks after the last concert of our first concert tour, little Johannes was born in Philadelphia. When our manager in New York heard about it he almost had a nervous breakdown. He never would have let me go on that long tour from concert to concert, and he complained bitterly at how I had outsmarted him. Three cheers for Mimi!

And so the months passed. The first concert tour was over and so was our visa, and the Trapp Family Singers were reminded to leave the country.

There we were with a six-week-old baby in the middle of March. We had three invitations to do concerts in the Scandinavian countries and so, on the power of these contracts, we received a visa for Denmark, Sweden and Norway—for one concert each.

We weren't even worried; we knew that this was the only thing for us to do, and God would provide. And He did! These three concerts finally turned into fifty-six performances throughout the Scandinavian countries—until September 30, 1939, when the war broke out.

Then our American manager sent us tickets for our next crossing so that we were able to fulfill our contract with him. Thank God, during the war, America did not expel anybody.

After the second concert tour we were able to pay back our initial debts, and lo and behold, there was a thousand dollars left! The other day I asked a banker, "How much would a thousand dollars in 1939 be worth today?"

He wasn't quite sure, but he thought it might be close to ten thousand dollars.

It was a lot of money for us. Now came the question, should we walk in our national costume into Macy's or Wannamakers' or Marshall Field's and come out in what we call civilian clothes? We felt so sorry to waste this hard-earned money on clothing, but at the same time we were so sick and tired of the constant traveling from hotel to hotel, with packing and unpacking, with the baby in the bus, that we decided in unison to continue wearing our Austrian outfits a little longer and buy a place of our own. So it was that we finally bought a farm in northern Vermont in the beautiful ski village of Stowe.

Until then we had believed that home could only be one spot on the globe—Austria. If you were so unlucky, so unhappy, to have lost your home, we thought you had to be homeless for the rest of your days. Now we discovered this was not so because home is where you belong, and having a little house on six hundred acres of Vermont soil made us belong again. Life for the Trapps took on a new meaning.

Then came the next hardship. The war was not over in half a year as everybody hoped and expected; it went on and on. Our two oldest sons, Rupert and Werner, were drafted. They chose the mountain ski troops.

For a moment it looked as though the Trapp Family Singers would have to stop their concert work. But we were very lucky to have as our manager F.C. Schang from Columbia Concerts, who had that rare quality—vision. Almost any other manager would have advised us to stop. Not so Freddy. With a glint in his eye which we learned to relish, he tackled the new situation. We gave it a try with our great musician, Father Wasner, who quickly reset the music for women's voices and one man's voice, and that became the war edition of the Trapp Family Singers.

The American audiences understood it fully. Soon after we had shed our initial shyness and stiffness on the stage and dared to smile, and even say a few words, we became quite popular, and Freddy Schang's pride and joy. He steered us safely into shortening our skirts from maxi to midi and loosening up our repertoire in order to take in a whole group of genuine folk songs from all lands. Finally Freddy became one of our closest friends. I just happen to remember, we never had a contract between him and us!

We usually traveled from September until after Easter, giving around a hundred concerts, and then we worked on our Vermont farm. We had learned the hard way that nobody should buy a house in "fair condition" because it may not be there the next time you come home. That is exactly what happened to us when the old farmhouse collapsed on our heads. Sleeping quarters for the girls had to be arranged in the loft of the horse barn in sleeping bags in the hay. My husband and I with little Johannes slept in one room above the kitchen, and Father Wasner was in the next one, while we were building the new house.

The years passed. Along came the Trapp Family Music Camp where we sang our own program with hundreds and hundreds of Americans, trying to introduce music to the families of America.

Then the war was over and both boys came home safe and sound. According to old Catholic tradition, they had made a vow: If they would come home safely from the war, they would build a chapel to "Our Lady of Peace" on the highest point of our property. And so it happened, and the chapel is now visited every year by hundreds of our guests.

Everything was looking up. The Trapp Family Singers had made a name for themselves from coast to coast, not only in America but also in Canada. The new house, a spacious Salzburger chalet, was finished. It has a porch on every floor and hundreds of window boxes which were full of flowers in the summer. (See photo section.)

The boys were back home and had begun to settle in their new lives. Rupert, the older, went on to medical school to repeat his examinations for his M.D., which he had received in Innsbruck shortly before we left Austria. Werner had started to get interested in running the farm.

Then the day came—on such a day one doesn't have to ask, "What is the will of God?" All one can do, all one must do, is say, "Thy will be done."

It was the day when God called our father.

The bishop in Burlington gave permission for us to have our own "God's Acre," the German word for cemetery, near the house under the trees, and from there the captain is still running the ship.

Again, time was rolling on. In 1950 the Trapp Family Singers were asked to sing in several foreign countries, beginning in Mexico, going through Central America and almost every country of Latin America, and finally back to Europe on a concert tour. By that time we had become American citizens.

When we had secretly left Austria we could tell only a very few chosen friends and relatives of our intentions, and they were all up in arms against it.

"Are you crazy?" they exclaimed. "Hitler has just promised a thousand years of peace. Don't you know what this means for your children? There are untold possibilities, and here you want to tear them out into an insecure future. This is wrong. You mustn't do it."

This was exactly what we hoped to hear, because we did not really want to go. It isn't easy to turn your back on everything and just walk out. All we needed was an excuse for staying, and this would be our excuse now. We could rightly say, "It is impossible that everybody else is wrong and we alone are right." We would stay.

But there is that certain something about wanting to do the will of God. If one is sincere and if one really wants to know what His will is, all one has to do is be quiet. Shut off television and radio, and in that silence one will always hear that still small voice in one's heart telling him what to do. We knew we had to go.

Now twelve years later, we went back on that European concert tour which took us into Austria. There were the same cousins and friends who had lost everything, and most of them had also lost their sons for Hitler. With very few words they admitted that we had done the right thing. That was a solemn moment in our lives.

Soon after the European concert tour, our children started to marry. Grandchildren started arriving, and we all knew that this was the beginning of the end of our singing group.

For twenty blissful years we had traveled the world together, bringing music to people and experiencing at every concert what a great peacemaker music is.

But we were called out once more, and that was in the year 1956. We sang every single day, with the exception of the days of travel, as we went to the other side of the world to Australia, New Zealand and the South Pacific.

And after our last concert in Sydney, Australia, when we thought that our work had come to an end, we began to see a new beginning.

10

A New Mission

In Sydney after our last concert we accepted an invitation to the home of Archbishop Carboni, who was the representative from Rome for all the mission stations in the South Pacific. After dinner he showed us movies and slides of the South Pacific islands, and we listened with rapt attention as he told us of the work among these people.

He had just returned from a long inspection trip and was very much concerned about the great success Communist agents were having all over that vast territory. After sharing these experiences with us, he faced us and simply asked, "When you are finished someday with your concert work, couldn't some of you come to the islands and start a lay missionary work among the people?"

A year later we answered his invitation. The first to go were three of my children, Maria, Rose Mary and Johanness. Archbishop Carboni wanted our priest friend and conductor, Father Wasner, and myself to travel for a year throughout the many islands to find out just exactly what was going on and what could be done about it.

So we went first to New Guinea, the land of mystery. In the very first week I learned to my utmost surprise that 711 languages are spoken there, each tribe having its own.

The neighboring tribes were usually enemies, and the tribes did not mix and neither did the languages. A common name for the natives in the jungle is *bush kanaka*, meaning something very low.

After we had traveled by boat, jeep, small aircraft and on foot from tribe to tribe, we came to Budoya, where my three children had worked for six months with Father Atchison. They were still very busy learning the language—Dobu.

These Melanesian languages are very intricate. For instance, whereas we have one English word for red or pink, there might be thirty Melanesian words describing colors from the palest pink to the darkest red. Or when we say, "We go," that could mean any number from two on. They have different words for "we," indicating the two of us alone and not a third present, or, or, or.

My three were very happy indeed. Maria and Rose Mary were teaching the little ones and going to the villages on "sick calls" while Johannes was working with the men and learning to build with native material. By and by he built a new church, two schoolhouses, and several smaller buildings. In his free time he went fishing and hunting wild pigs with the native boys.

Those few weeks on Father Atchison's station were most valuable for us. On many long evenings we told him what we had seen and experienced and then we listened to him.

He was a true godsend—first for his own people, and now for us—because he had used his twenty years in the bush—and hard years they had been—learning to "sit on the sand with them." After much listening this way, he learned to understand their own culture and to respect it.

One day he said very simply, "I finally found out that they have never experienced any real love but a lot of revenge and hatred and fear in their lives. If I wanted to preach Christ's words, "Love you one another as I love you," I was the one that had to first show them that love by becoming Christ for them." And this he surely did.

My children were so fortunate indeed to learn under such a master. But just as we had started to taste the adventure of the hidden treasure behind the word New Guinea, it was time for us to say good-bye and to go on.

Next we stopped over in Rabaul. Ten miles away on the edge of the jungle is Vunapope, a large mission station where we made friends with the late Bishop Scharmach. He told us right away that he wasn't interested in our lay program, as he had plenty of sisters and brothers working with him, but he was the most gracious host and had us stay for several weeks. During the days he sent us around to many outstations, and in the evenings he entertained us with the most hair-raising stories from the time of the Japanese invasion. From the other missionaries we heard how fearlessly he had defended his own. He was regarded as a true hero.

We arrived at the next island around noon, and a car was waiting to drive us out to the main mission. As usual I said good-bye to Monsignor Wasner, who disappeared in the priest's house while I was taken to the convent with the sisters. There were six elderly sisters, all of them from Germany, and they were very happy to have a guest with whom they could speak German. The Mother Superior showed me around and I was quite impressed with the nice native hospital the sisters had built up out of nothing. The various huts had big names like the Men's Ward, the Maternity Ward, etc.

How often I have said back home now, "Since I

have been in the Pacific I don't believe in germs any-more."

Their large sickrooms—dormitories actually—had earthen floors on which the cots were standing. When showing me his hospital during the day, the bishop said, "We have 100 beds. How many people do you think are sleeping here?"

Of course if I'm asked a question like this I sense there is a trick somewhere, so I said curiously, "I don't really know; I guess between 500 and 600."

"Come tonight and I'll show you" was the bishop's answer.

A patient will arrive at the hospital with his whole family and his own sweet potatoes and taros. In the evening this is quite a sight. Between the beds little fires are made on the earthen floor, and there every family cooks its own evening meal. Afterward they stretch out under the bed of their sick father or broth-er, at right angles to the patient.

"Ah—that's why the beds stand so far apart," I mused.

"Exactly," the bishop said dryly.

In this atmosphere of unsterilization, the women have their babies, those who have just undergone op-erations come from the operating room, and all go home safe and sound without infection. Aren't we white people perhaps a little too fussy?

As we came to the Men's Ward, a large hut with only one patient in it, the sister said to me, "He's the son of our high chief. A few days ago his friends brought him on a litter. They make them quickly out of native vine, and he was in an agony of pain. Sister Clara, the head nurse who is as good as three doctors in one, examined him and said, 'If it is a kidney stone we have to send him as soon as possible to the big hospital. But I'll try first. Maybe it is only small stuff which I can get rid of for him here.'

"And then she made him drink nonstop one whole gallon of water. She knew the tremendous pressure might force out whatever infectious small material might be in the kidney. Of course it couldn't remove a sizable kidney stone, but it usually takes care of sand and small gravellike stones. Sure enough, in a rather short time the poor patient began to moan and groan —it had worked. After a lot of passing of blood, the foreign matter departed from him and he was on his way to recovery."

The sister asked me whether I would like to visit a little bit. She said the young man had gone to school, was very intelligent, and spoke quite good English. With this she left me alone with the patient.

We had a most delightful little visit. Not only was he obviously very intelligent and quite well read, but he was a "joy to behold." His bronze-colored healthy young body only covered with a loincloth *laplap* could have served Michelangelo as model for his figure of young David. His features were very regular and, with his beautiful dark eyes and his mouth full of blinding white teeth constantly showing in a big smile, it was a pleasure to look at him.

Suddenly his smile disappeared and, with an expression of real terror, he stared at something behind me while at the same time the room darkened. The only opening was a wide door which was now partly filled with the body of a tremendously big, very dark, native.

I just had time to scramble to my feet before the man threw himself with one jump from the doorstep onto the cot, twisting the boy's body around with one grip. Fastening his lips to a spot on the youth's back, he started to make loud sucking noises. Then jumping up, he took from his mouth a long, thin green thread from a climbing vine, unrolling it in front of the terrorized eyes, and saying, "Here is your sickness; I took it out."

And then, holding out his hands, he added, "Three pounds." That amount of money represented the earnings of three months.

All this happened in less than two minutes. The horrified boy searched under his pillow, where he had obviously hidden his money. With a shaking hand he paid three pounds, whereupon the dark person disappeared.

"That was our medicine man. He is bad," whispered Nala-Nala, the son of the chief. After this he fell silent and didn't want to talk anymore.

I practically ran back to the sisters to tell them what I had just witnessed.

"Oh, was he here again?" exclaimed Sister Clara in dismay. "He is doing this all the time, taking the money away from our patients the moment we turn our back. He is so evil that the people obey him out of fright. He has such terrible black magic and, because the people believe it really works, he can paralyze them; if he leaves them paralyzed long enough, some even die. They are so deadly afraid of him."

Suddenly Sister Clara looked up with an expectant smile and said, "We can't do anything from here because he might burn down our whole station, but perhaps you could do something when you go back to the city."

And I did. A few days later I asked to be received by the head of the government, a high Australian official, and I told him the gruesome stories about this medicine man. Weeks later I received a triumphant letter from Sister Clara, telling me that the medicine man had been inducted into the army.

While I was sitting at the convent with the sisters, a boy came running over from the priest's house inviting the white lady to say hello to Father.

I went right along. When I had come around the small outcrop of jungle on the other side of which the church and the priest's house were situated, I saw that this was not only to say "hello" to Father. Obviously a big reception was going on. A very large group of natives was milling around between church and rectory —Presbytery, as it is called there.

Monsignor Wasner came over to me smiling. "Father has summoned the whole big village and wants us to listen to a concert. They are going to sing 'Ave Maria' by Schubert for us," announced the missionary proudly.

And so they did. I don't know why it made me so sad, but spontaneously I said to the interpreter (by then I had learned never to address a man directly!) to ask the big chief whether we could hear something from their own old chants.

The reaction was terrific. The big chief, the father of the patient I had visited just an hour before, was just as handsome as his son, with very expressive features. He was now obviously holding council with his men and, turning to the interpreter, sent the polite invitation to the Monsignor and myself to be at their village at a quarter to four. And then the whole crowd dispersed.

"I like that," Father Jim chuckled. "A quarter of four. Don't believe for a moment they know when that is. They simply heard us say that once. You may be in for a long wait."

And then he added, "There hasn't been a native chant on this island for the last three generations— ever since the Methodist missionaries came and quenched all that, which was just as well because all

109

they knew to sing about was love and war. That's why I taught them the 'Ave Maria' by Schubert."

It was around noon or early afternoon when I said good-bye in order to go back to the nuns. Father Wasner called out to me, "Let's be on time."

So at a quarter to four sharp we entered the big village, just the two of us, Monsignor Wasner and myself.

I had already learned that this big village was one of those arrangements where a whole tribe of five or maybe six hundred people stays together in one settlement. By now we had seen many similar villages. Usually we could hear the noise from afar—the barking of dogs, the voices of women shouting from house to house, the wailing, laughing and crying of babies. That's why it struck us so strangely that this village was so completely silent. It was like a ghost town.

As we walked through the street and peeked into different huts, there wasn't a soul around. Usually there would be old people or mothers with very young babies left behind, even if everybody else had gone hunting or fishing. But no, not even a dog was there.

After searching a while we went down to the beach, where Father Wasner took out his book to say vespers and I entertained myself by watching the sand crabs rushing around sideways. Almost an hour had passed when Father Wasner suddenly looked up from his book and said, "Can you hear something?"

I strained my ears at first to hear a very distant rumble, but then everything happened so fast that before I could even say yes, it had descended upon us. The distant rumble, like the sound of faraway breakers on the reef, reached an immense crescendo and then turned into an indescribable sound. It was not a howl; it was not a song. It was up-and-down scales of the weirdest kind, and the strongest force of many,

many voices. It was as I said, *indescribable*—but bloodcurdling. Then they came—rushing out of the jungle—the whole tribe in full gallop heading for us. Involuntarily we walked a few steps back when the chief, who was leading the stampede, suddenly halted a few steps in front of us, and his people stopped dead in their tracks. One could almost feel the shock of the airwaves as they stopped.

They had obviously retired into the jungle to get dressed, or perhaps I should say undressed. When we had gathered earlier to hear the "Ave Maria" by Schubert, the women had worn all kinds of cotton dresses and the men had on their usual *laplap*, the loincloth. But now they wore nothing but paint. They were painted in four different patterns. Some were adorned with intricate tattoos; these were the minor chiefs and their sons. The chief was simply covered with the most intricate tattoo pattern. With all that paint on, they didn't appear to be naked. One group of them, however, was painted all in white, and they kept in the background. Later we saw why.

The chief called out a command at which a few husky men rolled over some things which were obviously meant to serve as "stools" for us. Segments of a freshly cut tree, they were about a foot and half high. With the innate taste and politeness of the native people which I have encountered so many, many times, the chief surmised quite rightly that for Father and myself it wouldn't have been easy to squat on our haunches, the natural posture for his own people. Therefore, we were motioned to take our seats. The chief took his place next to Father Wasner and, while he gave the running account of what was to come, in pidgin English, Father had to turn each time and repeat it to me.

It would have been in very bad taste if I had said,

"Thank you very much, but I can understand the chief very well myself." This was protocol. A woman can never be addressed directly—only through a middle person.

Then the chief again said a few things in his native tongue and, turning to us, explained, "We are going to act out the history of our people for you."

A make-believe chief appeared, summoned the men, and said, "One, two, three, four, five . . . nineteen, twenty," touching each time some of the men on the shoulder.

"You go fishing," he ordered.

The same thing happened a few more times with other groups.

"You go hunting.

"You go building.

"You go watching."

"Watching whom or what?" asked Father Wasner.

"Our enemies, so that nobody comes who wants to eat us," said the chief.

Of course the production was back a few generations in the time when the area had been one of the most feared cannibal sections in the islands.

The chief invited us to follow him from group to group. We went over to the hunters, who had their bows and arrows. In no time they had shot birds in flight. Immediately they plucked the feathers and cleaned out the insides, made a fire by rubbing a little vine against some hard wood, and started to broil the birds on a green stick. It was marvelous.

Then we followed the chief over to the fishermen. This was a sight I shall never forget. Each one of them produced his spear, got in his canoe—a hollowed-out tree trunk—and paddled a little way offshore. There he stood motionless in the canoe like a figure made of bronze, wielding his spear above his head as he watched the moving fish in rapt attention until one big enough for his taste happened to come near. With lightning speed, down came the spear, and with a war whoop he lifted up his catch.

Over we went to the builders. On all of the islands the termites and the white ants are busily eating away on the native material of which the huts are built—palm trunks, palm thatch on the roofs, and handwoven mats covering the walls. Thus a house is usually good for only five years. The people have a marvelous rotation plan, and somebody is always getting a new house, with everybody, of course, pitching in to help construct the new building.

In no time the builders cleared their site, prepared stilts which they ran into the ground, and laid small trees across them to form the floor, taking care to leave air space between each tree. In the tropics, fresh-air ventilation and circulation are very important.

In the meantime groups of women were busily preparing palm leaves and "sewing" them with vines into sections which would eventually serve for the thatching of the roof. Other women were weaving new mats to go on the inside of the walls.

Great joy and happiness pervaded all this activity. We could hear singing and joking and, even though we didn't understand what was being said, we understood the spirit of joy, easiness, and uninhibited gaiety.

A short hour may have passed when suddenly someone from the group of watchers shielded his eyes, stared into the distance, and then uttered one of those spine-chilling cries.

The chief said quietly to Father Wasner, "The white men are coming."

All the people ran to the coast. Of course, no one was coming, but with incredible mimicry they pictured

113

perfectly the arrival of a rather large boat, visibly an outrigger canoe, as they helped to guide it in. Suddenly the white-painted people we had seen earlier were emerging from the background. They were the "white men" coming ashore.

The natives looked friendly and were in rapt attention at these strange white figures. Then they wanted to impress them, so they performed one of their chants.

But the white people immediately held their ears and said, "Oh, stop it! Stop it!"

From then on I honestly wished I didn't have to see the rest because the white people went over to the first hut, pointed at it, and said, "No good."

Then they produced corrugated iron and showed the natives that this was the thing to put on the roof. Next they approached the women, shielding their eyes, and said disgustedly, "Naked! Oh, oh!" and produced cotton clothes.

And then, if I hadn't been so sad I would have laughed aloud. From somewhere a thing was produced and put in the middle of the group. Once upon a time it had been a cotton dress. But obviously it had been worn day and night, night and day, until so much sweat had permeated it that by now it was standing all by itself without anyone inside. Quickly vines were strung between the huts. The women were shown by the white men how to wash the rags and then hang them over the vines. The beautiful native village had turned into a slum.

Next, the people started to cough. Unaccustomed to sweating and then lying around in wet rags, by and by they all caught colds and finally pneumonia. The story closed as the people lay on their faces and the chief went up and said, "All dead. The end."

At this everybody jumped to his feet and crowded

around most happily, not even guessing what a shattering impression they had left with us. I felt so humiliated and so sad because there was so much truth involved. But there was nothing one could do to turn back the wheel of history.

I told Father Wasner to tell the chief that this had been one of the greatest hours of my life and that I would pray to God that the end would be as it had been pictured. I wished him God's choicest blessings, to which Father Wasner added his own congratulations, and in deep thought we started to walk back to the station.

Suddenly I stopped Father Wasner and said, "And how about the medicine man? Why didn't they portray this important personage in their people's life? The way they did it, it looks to us like *Paradise Lost*, but I have met the serpent."

Father Wasner slowly turned and walked back. Days later he told me in the plane that he had had a private heart-to-heart talk with the chief, who finally admitted shyly that he was just beginning to see the power of the Lord Jesus over their evil spirits and the medicine man.

11

The Native Chant

One of the things I really love to do with almost a passion is to swim. At the drop of a hat I'm in any water which is available. I don't swim fast but I can swim forever. And there I was in New Guinea, traveling from one coastal station to the other, always on the ocean. Of course my first wish upon arriving at a new station was: "May I go for a swim?"

I was always put up in the house with the sisters. So at the first mission station the Reverend Mother said, "Oh, no! That's not possible here. The water is full of sharks."

So back went my bathing suit into the suitcase.

A few days later I arrived at another station and said, "Now, let me go for a swim."

"Oh, for heaven's sake, no!" the Reverend Mother said. "Here the big crocodiles are just waiting to bite your leg or arm off."

With a big sigh, again in went my bathing suit.

Again a few days later, on an especially hot day after I was taken in at a very friendly new convent, I swung my bathing suit over my shoulder and announced my intention. Reverend Mother threw up her hands.

"But we have an underwater current here. It's very dangerous. Nobody can go swimming."

At the fourth station I didn't say a word. I sneaked

119

out in my bathing suit and ran into the water. I remember distinctly that I was all by myself as I dove through the breakers. But when I came out on the other side, I suddenly saw thirty or forty black heads bobbing up and down with me in the surf. In this particular bay the water was really infested with sharks, and the women of the village, who had been watching me, had all come to my rescue.

The natives have an unerring way of shying sharks away. With their left hand they make something like the figure eight under the water. When at a certain moment the left hand swings over the right hand, this produces a vacuum, the result is an explosionlike sound which keeps the sharks at a distance.

My children are very handy and can do almost anything which can be done with ten fingers. But Maria, Rose Mary and Johannes, on their mission station which was also on the ocean, have tried time and again throughout the years to learn that particular gesture under water and have never succeeded.

Finding myself surrounded by my bodyguards and, having picked up pidgin English enough to converse, we had a wonderful time in the water. After about half an hour I had had enough, so I went to the shore. As I arrived out of the waves, the houseboy came running down from the convent, carrying a chair which he placed in front of me as he said in pidgin English, "Reverend Mother sends the chair for the white queen to sit on."

Staring at him in disbelief, I said, "Will you bring the chair back to Reverend Mother? I will sit on the sand."

As he walked back home with his chair, I noted that all the women had watched me in breathless attention. I mingled with them as they all came crowding in on me, and we sat together as one happy bunch on the wet sand of the South Pacific.

Suddenly an old lady said, "I'm sorry. Somebody has died in your family."

I said with a start, "I hope not. Why?"

"But you are painted all white."

I didn't quite know what she meant until she pointed to my skin. Then I realized there was a funny pattern between my tanned skin and where I had usually worn a blouse and skirt which protected me from the sun. The difference between the darkly tanned portion of my body and the rest of my skin was rather striking.

I had already learned that the natives paint their bodies white with lime after a death occurs in their family, because there has always been something in the past—some little disagreements, some fights, some bad words going back and forth—and they believe the spirit of the deceased person remembers this and can come back to haunt them. But if they are painted white they think the dead man's spirit will not recognize them. After four weeks they believe he will have completely forgotten about them, so then they can wash themselves in the ocean. So that is what the people thought of my funny "paint."

I insisted that I was not painted, so the lady who had spoken first said, "May I try?"

And I said wonderingly, "Yes, of course."

There she was, as quick as a bunny, licking at the white spots of my skin. Some of the other more daring ones tried also.

I could have shrieked because it tickled so much. Very soon I turned pink from the licking, but it was a key which opened a door usually closed tightly to white people. I was admitted, so to say, into the family. I became like one of them, sitting with them on the sand and letting myself be licked and handled.

I used this precious situation to ask them three very personal questions pertaining to cutting events in their life. What do you do when you have a baby? What do you do when you get married? What happens if somebody dies? I'm very grateful that this experience occurred early in my missionary year, because I used the same type of situation time and again to learn more about the people.

Once again we were picked up by a mission plane. This time we were carried to northern New Guinea to Wewak, very close to the equator. As we arrived at the airport a tall, slender missionary approached us with outstretched hands and introduced himself as Bishop Arkfeld from Iowa. One look into his good eyes assured me that this man was different. He was as Christ walking among his people. And for three happy weeks we reaffirmed this again and again.

The bishop had already heard about our intention to start a lay missionary movement and he was most eager to help us. Therefore, he flew us himself to each one of his mission stations, which were partly on the coast, partly upstream on the river, and partly in the highlands. Bishop Arkfeld is the most renowned pilot in that section, and he has government permission to use any landing strip at his own discretion.

We experienced all kinds of things with him in his little Cessna. Once there was an airstrip which started uphill. The bishop was already seated behind the instruments, and I was behind him with Father Wasner. The bishop sent a native boy to look at the upper part of the landing strip for cows.

The boy came running back and said, "No cows, Bishop."

He turned on the machine and took off. But as he

rolled up the landing strip, it was simply covered with pigs! He just barely made it.

He turned quietly to us and said, "It's my fault. I only asked about cows."

Those weeks we spent in his territory on the Sepik River will always remain among the most mysterious experiences of my life. There we were in the region of the ghost houses. As we approached from the airport, the bishop pointed out a village. In the middle of the village was a ghost house—the House Tambaran.

I remember vividly my first acquaintance with a ghost house. The airstrip is usually a distance away from the village and, as we wound our way through the jungle toward the huts, I saw splotches of red on the ground. I had an eerie feeling that this might be blood and perhaps even human blood. Then suddenly we came out of the jungle and there was the village, neatly arranged in a semicircle, and sitting in the middle was the House Tambaran—the ghost house—with its steeple. The entire ground in front of the ghost house was dark red.

The bishop must have seen the shudder in my eyes because he suddenly broke out in a broad smile and said, "Betel nut!"

Right there and then I learned that the men were carrying a gourd filled with powdered lime around with them and, as they chewed the betel nut, they mixed it with the lime, which turned their saliva to a foamy blood-red. This was spat artfully around. Well, I certainly did feel relieved.

Then the bishop pointed at the vine which hung down from the top of the steeple to about mouth height. He said the men would come and whisper their petitions at the end of the vine, and they believed the petition would travel up into the ghost house.

With great ceremony, I was ushered into the house

itself. That was a great rarity, a very big exception, because women are forbidden by penalty of death to enter a ghost house. Even if they pass it they shade their eyes in order to not look directly at it. As we stood within the house in the twilight, some light seeped in through the plants and reeds which formed the outside wall. We could see hanging from the roof, suspended on vines, a huge five-foot-long taro root, their sacred fruit. It reminded me instantly of the holy Eucharist in our churches. What bread is to us, taro is to them. It is their daily bread, and this particular taro was their holy bread. There was a direct connection of worship. Reverently, all of us left the ghost house.

The more I experienced going from station to station, the more I appreciated the reverence of Bishop Arkfeld toward the customs of his people. He never belittled them, never talked down to them. He always accepted them for what they were, gently turning their old cultures toward the light of Christianity. No wonder he was loved like a father by his people.

Once we came to a village on the Sepik River. As usual upon arrival, we distributed first aspirin and then Nivaquin, the antimalarial pill. We all dressed their wounds and listened to their stories before the missionary announced a service of holy mass. He reminded me very much of the time when our Lord was walking the earth and He first healed the sick and helped the blind, the deaf and the lame before preaching the word and later offering the sacrifice of His life.

In this particular village the people had been most eager for us to come. Suddenly the big chief announced with a strong voice the lifting of the big taboo. A murmur went around his people. The bishop bent down to me and whispered, "He has lifted the taboo for the women. He has thrown open the House

Tambaran. He wants the Christian service to be performed in it."

At that moment the chief had called out several other orders. And then came the hour I will never forget.

On the Sepik River the drums are very important. They are for the House Tambaran what church bells are for our churches. There are drums of all sizes, hollowed out of tree trunks, and the largest ones have to be manned by two men with big clubs. The tree trunk might be three or four feet in diameter and nine feet long, hollowed out with continuous labor for many months, or maybe years, through a five-inch-wide slit. As the big club hits the hollow trunk it gives a booming sound like a very low bell of a cathedral in Europe. The drums vary in size from the biggest, which might be twelve feet long, to the smallest, which might be only two feet long, with a very high-pitched tone. The chief announced that from then on the drum signal normally used for battle for attacking another tribe would now only be sounded as a battle cry against the evil spirits and in honor of the "Christian God."

Now, with all the people—including us—standing at attention, it began: *boom-boom*. Strong men hit the big drum with full force, and then, gradually, the other drums joined in, until finally the very air reverberated with an incredible sound which cannot be described but had to be heard. Suddenly the chief raised his hand; it all stopped.

For a few minutes everyone stood rooted to the ground. Then the chief invited everybody—really *everybody*—for the first time into the ghost house. There the holy sacrifice of the mass was celebrated on the ground where human sacrifice had been brought two or three generations earlier. It was a solemn moment.

Afterward the chief showed us around. For the first

time I saw huge long pipes, three feet in diameter, of native woven material like that used in their mats. We were told that the mosquitoes were very bad, so this was a substitute for our mosquito netting. A whole family would sleep in such a tube or pipe. Of course, there was hardly any air to breathe inside, but it was still more endurable than being enveloped in a cloud of mosquitoes as everybody is during the day. The smell of those tubes was indescribable.

Then came the great day when the bishop announced, "And now we are going up to the highlands to the headhunter country. I mean," he added hastily, "where the people have been headhunters."

Then, with a twinkle in his eye, he again added, "Now it is almost extinct."

The way he pronounced "almost" spoke volumes.

The little Cessna climbed and climbed and soon we were flying across the jungle and unbroken green carpet below. One couldn't see a house or a field or a garden—nothing but jungle. After an hour or so, the bishop pointed ahead and said, "Can you see the airstrip?"

By straining my eyes I could barely distinguish an area the shape of a towel in a lighter green than the jungle.

"Well, that's it," said the bishop.

Sure enough, very soon he circled the green towel and landed. At the moment of landing we were completely alone. But in the very next moment we were surrounded by people, all jabbering happily together as they greeted their good friend the bishop.

As I hopped out of the little airplane I noticed that the nylon stocking on my right leg had kind of spiraled around and around. Instinctively I bent over, with my fingers between stocking and leg, and straightened it out.

The response was absolutely deafening. While the bishop had told us a good number of things about the customs of the headhunters, he had completely forgotten to mention what they do when they are astonished. While we would say, "no, not really," they make a sound which is hard to describe. It is a gargling hollow droning noise which is absolutely bloodcurdling to the uninitiated ear, even when made by only one voice. Multiply this by 300 and it's obvious why I was completely shaken.

Headhunters! I thought. *This is it!*

Oh, no, these people were only astonished. An interpreter came over and politely said in pidgin English, "White queen, please do it again."

"Do *what* again?" I asked, astonished.

"Please wiggle your skin for us again."

During the next hours I could see, behind bushes and trees, the young headhunter maidens trying desperately to imitate me "wiggling my skin."

These people in the highlands were still living in the stone age. In one of the stations I was the first white woman they had ever seen. They had seen some white men from the government and a missionary or two, but never a white woman, so I was an absolute sensation.

Usually the bishop himself piloted us to his outstations, although once in a while we flew with one of his other pilots. But every time, after a few days' stay, we returned to the main station again to "talk things over."

Once we were sitting in the bishop's house having breakfast with him when a native boy came running in. Panting and obviously terribly excited, he talked in a high-pitched voice in his native language, which the bishop spoke like his own.

From the agitation on the bishop's face, we saw that

something important must have happened. The bishop turned to us.

"High up on the Sepik River, one village has eaten another village."

Just like that. While the government is working very hard on extinguishing cannibalism in those far, faraway places, it was still going on. The story went like this:

One village had sent messengers to another village, declaring their intention to celebrate a peace treaty. This was eagerly received by their former foes, and the whole population appeared in their canoes without weapons. Unfortunately it had only been a very shrewdly laid-out trap, and the helpless people were simply slaughtered.

This was a serious event, and this time the church and the government wanted to go together and explain to the tribe that "we don't do things like this anymore."

It's rediculous to punish people for doing something which is a part of their culture and tradition. The cannibal doesn't eat his fellowman only for the sake of eating; this is a part of his religion. For by getting a bite of his fellowman, he believes he immediately inherits some of that person's strength; and if he sucks some of the brain out of the skull, he thinks he will inherit some of the dead man's spirit.

A small expedition was put together, including government officials and several missionaries. Monsignor Wasner and I were invited to join them. It was a chance in a lifetime.

While that trip was one of the most interesting experiences, it was also one of the most painful. I have to describe what it means to be paddled up the Sepik River in a native canoe. The natives in this part of the New Guinea are rather small, around four feet and

My father.

My mother.

Maria and father
"on one of those trips."

Maria—age five.

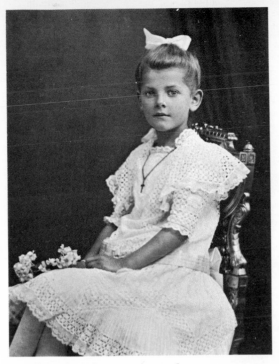

Maria's confirmation.

Villa Trapp—Salzburg, Austria.

Maria as the new Baroness.

Johannes.

Georg von Trapp.

*The Baron
and son Johannes.*

Maria's new family.

Maria at the
State Teachers School
of Progressive Education.

Maria and Georg.

Lorli and Rosemarie.

*We worked
together to build
our home, "Cor Unum,"
in Stowe, Vermont.*

*Never buy a house
in fair condition.*

"Cor Unum" in summer.

The "Trapp Family Singers."

The "bay" window.

Maria and native child.

Baron von Trapp
lighting the Advent wreath.

very slim. The canoe is a hollowed-out tree trunk made to size, and I was simply stuffed into one and couldn't move.

But that was only one of the pains. The Sepik River has vast stretches of swampland on both sides where the Kunai grass grows up to twelve feet tall. This is simply the home of the mosquitoes. During all our waking hours we were enveloped in a cloud of mosquitoes. I still remember with disgust that constant high-pitched *whirr* and that constantly recurring little prick. Finally I found myself wishing for some decent pain—something like kidney stones, for instance. But there was nothing I could do but wait until sunset.

Then the canoe would land at the nearest village. We all would walk up to the "house government," a native hut reserved for visitors and fortified with mosquito netting. There in our mosquito-net cubicles we could eat our one big meal a day in peace and seclusion. In no time the net would be covered with angry mosquitos shrieking out their fury at not being able to get at us.

We had hardly left the coast in our canoes when the people in the village for which we were heading knew about our coming. The message goes via the bush telephone—the drummer. Certain natives have the telegraph service hanging around their necks on a vine. It is the *kundu*, a little three-foot drum on which they tap. The drums are strategically located throughout the jungle. One drummer picks up the message from the other and, while it took us five days and five nights to get to the place, the message traveled the entire distance in less than half an hour.

This reminds me of a funny incident in the beginning of my missionary trip. It was also in the highlands but on the other side of New Guinea. The missionary we were visiting then was a German priest, Father

129

Schilling, later Bishop Schilling. As I was walking with him through the jungle to get to the next village, I heard drumming from afar. This being a new sound to me, it was rather spine-chilling.

Immediately thinking of all the stories I had read about drum signals being war signals, I said, "Father, do you understand what it says?"

Father Schilling said, "Yes, I do."

"What is it saying?"

"Oh, nothing. Nothing really," said Father Schilling.

Obviously he didn't want to tell me the terrible message going through the jungle. But I begged him so long that he finally with a little sigh told me that the goods from Sears, Roebuck had arrived at the mission station. He knew he had destroyed some expectancy on my part.

Finally the ordeal was over and we neared the village in question. As these people had been minutely notified by the drums of every one of our movements, all the men had to do about half an hour before our arrival was to retire into the jungle. So when we arrived there wasn't one single man to be seen, only women. It was now up to the government officials and the natives they had brought from the coast to find and persuade the men out of the jungle in order to give them a talking to. Suddenly I found myself alone with the women—really a chance of a lifetime. The victorious chief had twenty-five wives, and one is wife number one, the first lady.

I couldn't help but ask her in pidgin English, "How does it taste?"

She gave me the New Guinea answer for "the best of the best" by sucking in her breath and crossing her eyes.

I asked my second question: "Which parts are best?"

She pointed to the inside of the lower forearm, the cheeks, the palms of the hands and the calves.

That left me with one more unanswered question: "How about where we sit?"

The first lady frowned and very disgustedly said, "Much too tough. Has to be smoked."

This was true New Guinea dialogue.

The return trip was made rather quickly. In two days we were back home on the main station because we went downstream and the paddling natives outdid themselves because they also like to return home.

Once more the bishop flew us up to the highlands to leave us there for a native feast. He said he would pick us up in three days. It was around full moon. I learned to appreciate something in the middle country: the moon. The sun was completely uninteresting; every day it rose at 6 A.M. and set at 6 P.M. There was only a very little variation of about twenty minutes one way or another.

But the moon! There she comes—a tiny sliver on the evening sky—and there she glows every day until she finally shines in her full resplendent majesty, turning night into day. Full moons are not for sleeping. Children are playing and running around, dogs are barking, ladies are sitting around their fires, telling stories until the wee hours until it's hardly worthwhile to get a few winks of sleep. And then—oh horror. There she is waning. Every day you see a little less of her, and then comes the horrible night when she shines no more. Real depression settles over all the tribes. Although they have experienced it month after month throughout their lives and throughout their history, somehow one can never be quite sure: Will she come again?

One evening stands out in my memory. We had attended evening devotions with my children in their station at Budoya. It must have been in May. After we came out of the service, all of us stood around with the people on the big lawn in front of the church, surrounding Father Atchison who had come out to join us. Suddenly someone pointed to the sky, and the whole large crowd of between 200 and 300 people made a tremendous sound which rose like the roaring of the breakers out on the reef. It can't be described, but it can be imitated by opening your mouth wide and uttering just one loud sound but clapping your mouth shut quickly with your hand. But then don't forget to multiply it by 200. It certainly was startling to me until Father Atchison came over and with a big smile pointed to the sky. I really had to squint to see her—the tiny sliver of the moon. Here she was back again; life was going on.

I arrived in New Guinea with the largest suitcase permitted on a train or plane. Since we were stopping in Australia and had to be prepared for winter, I had brought a lot of warm clothing. And for New Guinea there were my summer things, plus various books, a little jewelry, and all kinds of everyday necessities without which we of the twentieth century think we can't exist.

Then I made this wide trip throughout many centuries back into the stone age. Every time I was invited to a chief's house I brought presents. First my winter things. Then all kinds of little boxes in which I stored my paraphernalia. My huge suitcase got lighter and lighter and emptier and emptier. When there were only two light summer dresses and a little underwear left besides my Bible and a big red hankerchief, I decided to fold my belongings right into the handkerchief, which I knotted and fastened to a stick, while I gave my suitcase to Chief Iad in exchange for a dagger made of a human thigh bone with the joint as a handle.

"Muchly used," assured the chief.

Then he added quickly, "By my ancestors."

His much-beloved baby was playing around his legs when suddenly he grabbed him, put him in the suitcase, closed it, and sat on it. I had the hardest time to get him off it before the baby suffocated. Quickly I tore the lid off and took it with me, again to exchange it in the next village for a breastplate made with stone tools out of mother of pearl.

These last weeks, when I owned only the bare essentials, belonged to the happiest time of my life.

And then our year of exploration had come to an end. Monsignor Wasner and I went to see the Apostolic Delegate in Sydney and gave him a detailed account of our experiences. We told him my children intended to stay on at their station, which they did. Johannes left after three and a half years to go to college. Rose Mary returned home after five years and went into nurse's training. Maria stayed on; this is her tenth year.

Monsignor Wasner had become so entranced with the great need and the great possibilities of mission work that he accepted the invitation of the Bishop of Fiji to become a missionary in Naiserelangi. For seven years he did outstanding and very difficult work between the two ethnic groups, Fijians and Indians, before his health gave way. Soon afterward he was called to Rome and made a Papal Prelate. Now he is heading the House of Studies at the German Parish in The Eternal City.

For twenty years he had been our musical director and our most faithful friend and helper. When my husband and I in 1938 had told our bishop in Salzburg of our intention to leave our home in order to get away from Hitler's tyranny, the bishop had advised Father Wasner right then and there to join us on this journey into the unknown.

I can remember how the old gentleman looked thoughtfully through his window over to the cupola of the cathedral and said, "It will prove one day to be of great importance that Father Wasner is leaving now."

That was a real prophecy, because without Father Wasner we never could have become the Trapp Family Singers who, after the war, collected daily, from every concert, anything that the kind-hearted Americans wanted to give for the poor people in Austria. It finally became possible for the Trapp Family Austrian Relief, Inc., to send over 275,000 pounds of goods into little war-torn Austria.

And so the time finally came when a small party, just Father Wasner and ourselves, was sitting for the last time around the family table. It was good-bye and Godspeed before Father Wasner left for Fiji.

"For twenty blissful years we had traveled the world together, bringing music to the people," I had said earlier as we had been reminded of those blissful years. We recalled how much blood, sweat and tears it had involved, how many sacrifices on everybody's part it had cost, to make those twenty years possible, because it hadn't been a normal life for the whole family to be so closely connected for that long a time. But when all was said and done, we all agreed: it had been worth it. And the old slogan, "A family that prays together, stays together," had proven true. And so our heartfelt thanks and grateful prayers would follow him wherever he went.

12

Repentence

After my husband's death I went through a time of terrible struggles. He died at the end of May, and I had all the month of June to think about things I had done and to cry my eyes out in repentance. I relived my entire married life.

I have a terrible temper, and I had thrown things across the room, yelled at the top of my voice, banged a door and, in order to make sure that he understood what I meant, had opened the door again and slammed it again.

My poor husband, being just the opposite of me, had stood in stunned silence. Instead of spanking me or doing something drastic, he just endured it; but then he would be crushed for days. When I had finished with my tantrum, I always felt so good that I didn't understand what was the matter with him. I would even say, "Darling, is anything bothering you?"

And he needed days to get over the hurt. In the meantime I had worked up the next hurricane.

So in the weeks immediately after his death, I relived all of these things over and over again—how I had acted in Kalamazoo, Michigan, or in Toronto, Canada, or in Chattanooga, Tennessee. There wasn't a city in the United States of America or, for that matter, anywhere else where I wondered if I might not have been nasty or ugly to my darling husband.

For hours I would just sit near his grave, begging his pardon and forgiveness. Gladly I would have dug him out with my own hands if I could have made him alive again, giving me another chance to be the way I wanted to be from now on. But it was too late. Those terrible words *too late* were really haunting me. I couldn't stop crying.

Then came July and the beginning of our music camp, and I couldn't afford to cry in the daytime. The campus was crawling with people, and they would come in a stupid and indelicate way and say, "Oh, I've heard your husband died. Is that true? How long ago? It must be lonesome without him. . . ."

"Oh, it's already four weeks ago," I would reply.

I wouldn't allow myself to cry, so I hardened myself and with absolute dry eyes and a dry tone of voice I answered these questions in a cool and objective way —until 11 o'clock at night when the whole campus was asleep and I turned out the main switch.

When I came back to the house where I lived by myself, I started crying and I couldn't stop. I cried and cried all through the hours of the night. Night after night this happened until my eyes were swollen. The skin under my eyes got sore, and finally the little blood vessels burst.

So I went to see our old country doctor nearby. He gave me a little white pill, I suppose a tranquilizer. Not only did it not help me; it made me crawl up the walls. It made me more nervous than just crying. So I went back to him and told him these little white pills were not helping me but making matters worse. He said, "I really think you should see a psychiatrist."

I had reached the end of my rope, so even a psychiatrist was all right with me. But I really didn't like the idea of going to a man, so I started searching for a woman psychiatrist. Someone gave me the New York

138

City address of a German refugee lady from Berlin. I made an appointment and went down to New York City.

As I entered her office, she greeted me warmly and said, "Now tell me your last dream."

"Oh," I said, "I never dream. I know from books that we all dream, but my dreams never come up to the surface. From January 1 through December 31, I have had no dreams."

"Then I can't help you," said the lady in an exasperated voice. "But wait a minute, maybe there is something."

And then she stared at a large stone figure standing on her desk. In a venerating kind of way she introduced me to the figure, saying, "This is an old sage from China. Maybe he can help us."

She picked up the three-foot heavy thing and put it down on the floor in front of her fireplace and motioned for me to sit next to her on the carpet.

So we sat there, and within minutes I felt a presence. I didn't see or hear anything; but I had a deep-down consciousness or someone being there, and this someone was eerie.

Suddenly I was so scared and frightened that I jumped to my feet, ran out of the room, down the stairs, out of the house, and all the many blocks from East 76th Street to West 55th Street to my good old Hotel Wellington. I ran into the hotel and right into the elevator which was on the verge of going up. And, funny enough, I didn't even pant. I was too tense. As I got out of the elevator I ran along the corridor to my room. At my bed I sank on my knees and cried out loud, "Georg, help me." (Georg being my husband.)

At that moment I remembered St. Joseph's Abbey in Spencer, Massachusetts.

Why in the world hadn't I thought of that before?

139

Reverend Father Abbott, my dearest and most helpful friend to whom I had opened my heart several times before, lived there. Now I was in a fix, and he surely would know what to do for me. So in a wild fury I stuffed all the things lying around into my suitcase, hurried downstairs, and did what I have never done before, called over to the desk: "Please send the bill."

I rushed out of the hotel right into a waiting taxi and said, "Grand Central Station."

I paid the taxi and, sure enough, within five minutes a train was leaving for Boston. I got off at Worcester, took a taxi, and within half an hour I was at St. Joseph's.

St. Joseph's Abbey is built on a crest of a long, sloping mile-long hill. At the foot of the hill is the Porter's Lodge where you have to stop and say what you want. So I got out and asked Brother Joseph, another old friend of mine, "Brother Joseph, please, I have to see Father Abbott."

"Sorry, Mother Trapp, Father Abbott left an hour ago for Chile."

My knees got soft and I sank into a chair, staring unbelievingly at Brother Joseph.

After a little while I said, "Brother Joseph, if something bothers you very much, who in this big abbey would you go see?"

And without a moment's hesitation, Brother Joseph said, "Only Father Raphael."

"Would you kindly ask him whether he has a moment's time?"

Brother Joseph did. Then he said, "He'll be right here."

Next to the Porter's Lodge stands an old little New England farmhouse which belongs to the abbey, and inside is a comfortable sitting room for women visitors. This is where Brother Joseph led me to wait. In no time the door opened and a white figure in a black scapula came in with a very friendly "Good afternoon, Mother Trapp."

Starting at the very end, namely, with the sage standing on the carpet and frightening me to death, I told Father Raphael my whole story. To the best of my knowledge, I tried not to overlook any one of those evil deeds by which I made my husband miserable.

When I was all through, Father Raphael looked at me so kindly and lovingly, as our Lord must have looked at some of those evil women he cast demons out of. There were very few questions and answers, and then he informed me that this had been a general confession over my whole life and he was now giving me absolution. That meant, he said, that not only God almighty in heaven, but also my dear husband who is now in God and loves me more than ever before, will have forgiven and forgotten all those sins.

Words cannot describe my peace and happiness as I floated out on a cloud, got in a taxi, and went back to New York and then back home, never to cry again, but to try now—as Father Raphael had admonished me—to undo the past damage by doing good from now on.

There is a little cemetery behind our house. From my room and from my balcony I can see it; it is just two hundred feet away. There I would go at the end of the day and talk over the day, the good and the bad, with Georg. Any day that I foresaw difficulties, I would go in the morning and ask his help and intervention. As he is now with God, he is so much more powerful to help me. While he was alive he wouldn't have hesitated to walk on foot to the West Coast if this had been a remedy in helping me when I was sick, for he really loved me. Now he doesn't have to walk to

141

the West Coast. He is so close to our heavenly Father that one glance will be a supplication. Many a time I have been asked whether it is not scary or whether I liked to have his grave that close. Well, in the beginning I even had a bench there, and I sat there by the hour. But then, people are funny. They thought this was a picnic ground, and every so often I had to pick up the orange peels and egg shells, and they were photographing each other on his grave. So we put a hedge around it.

Many a time we have talked about this in the family. Our father seems to be much closer now than before; the captain is still running the ship.

13

Trapp Family Lodge

Whenever I am at home in Stowe, Vermont, I go from table to table in the dining room each evening and greet our guests.

Once while on my way around a couple from Chicago stopped me and asked one of the most natural questions in the world: "How long have you had this lodge?"

And to my untold embarrassment, I looked stunned for a moment and then had to say truthfully, "You know what? I really don't know, but I'll tell you tomorrow."

It so happened that four of my children were home at that time, so after dinner I asked them to come for a little chat in my room. When they were there, I said, "Say, how long have we operated this place as a lodge? Some people asked me today, and I really felt stupid when I had to say I didn't know. Just when *did* we start?"

And so together we went back through the years.

We had never intended to have a lodge, a restaurant, a totel or anything of that kind, so how did we ever get into this? Many years ago we operated the "Trapp Family Music Camp" in the summer. From the very beginning we made it a rule that we took only participants, no onlookers. It happened time and time again that a nonsinging husband, or a nonsinging wife,

145

or grandmother or parents, or cousins, etc., came along. This goes back to the years during World War II, and at that time there were no places open in Stowe during the summer because Stowe was strictly a ski town. Therefore, we accommodated these extra people in our personal rooms which we had vacated in order to go down to the music camp. We lived at the camp and our rooms were empty, so we rented them. People loved it very much on our hill, so they would write asking whether they could come back during the fall or in the spring. In these years we were away on concert tours in the fall and in the spring, so again our rooms were empty. We had a very dear friend who was our cook and housekeeper, and she made these people feel at home. These rooms later developed into the Trapp Family Lodge.

In the year after my husband's death it was discovered that I had a brain tumor which had to be operated on; the doctor told me I had a fifty-fifty chance. I was a little bit worried. In case I didn't come back from the hospital, what were my poor children who had just lost their father to do? With both me and him missing, the concertizing would most likely not be continued. How could I provide for the future?

Our very close friend, "Uncle Craig," the man to whom we turned in all troubles and who helped us solve problems and answer questions, advised us to add another wing to the house.

"There is always snow in Stowe, you know," he said smilingly. "There will always be winter business here, and you can't go wrong in adding a few more beds."

That started the additions because, when it happened that I came back from the hospital safe and sound, the place soon proved to be still not big enough, so we added another wing. A few years later Johannes proved with pencil and paper that if we had twenty more rooms we could get out of the red in the winter, and the result was the so-called "Lower Lodge."

Now we had it all up-to-date, and as we were sitting there talking "Lodge" we went from one "Do you remember?" to the other.

We all agreed that the most comfortable time was twenty years ago in the beginning when we had only the original house which we built ourselves. At first one of our girls was our cook. As she went down the hill to continue cooking in the camp, "Tante Caro," a dear friend of the family, took over the kitchen in our house. She is also from Austria and a wonderful cook. Those were the days when there was only one menu and the guests sat around one large table. The soup was ladled out from a big tureen, and the other food was on platters, served family style. Everybody would help himself, and it was all very *gemutlich* (German for cozy, genial, comfortable).

In one corner of our living room is a famous bay window with a bench around the wall. After every meal, coffee would be served at a big table there, and the most heated discussions would transpire. I remember one year when somebody started with the question, "What is beautiful?" and from meal to meal the discussion was continued for weeks. It was most interesting that everyone had different ideas; but finally we all agreed that while taste may change as far as beauty goes, one thing was essential: whatever was called beautiful had to be perfect in its kind. This might differ completely between New Guinea, Hollywood and Stowe, Vermont, each one calling his object beautiful and perfect in its kind. Finally we arrived at the statement that beauty was in the eyes of the beholder.

All of us loved these sessions in the bay window. Then came the times of the additions to the house,

147

and that was the end of family style. The large dining table disappeared and many smaller tables took its place. Tante Caro said that while she had liked to cook for 20, when it was enlarged to 60, 80, 100—even up to 150—then it had become a real restaurant which called for a staff. And here begins the saga of the chef.

There are chefs and chefs—each one of them is a cook, some have a specialty in their own field, but usually each one of them has a weakness.

There are the ones who throw pots and pans in the air when they get nervous.

Others use unusable language.

Again, there are others who pinch the waitresses where they don't want to be pinched.

There were some who shopped for their own home cooking downstairs in our refrigerator.

Rather soon we got used to the fact that the new chef usually wanted to dispose of the former chef's pots and pans—made of aluminum—and demanded those made of copper. He also insisted on an electric deep-fryer. Quietly we would go to the garage where we had stored these exact items his predecessor had disposed of. It happened time and time again.

"Do you remember the one who made that deli-cious Hungarian goulash like no one else, with sixteen different ingredients?"

"Oh, yes, his name was Bob. But do you remember how one evening a gentleman wished to speak with him and, after a whispered conversation, Bob said 'excuse me' and went along with the gentleman who happened to be an agent of the FBI? Unfortunately Bob was 'wanted.'"

And so we chuckled along, having a wonderful time reminiscing, when somebody said, "But the crown and glory of them all was Chef Joseph."

Well! He certainly was somebody. He arrived with his own kitchen boy. He was big, broad-shouldered, with a ruddy face, and a big smile at all times. It was never so joyous in the kitchen as it was when Chief Joseph was there. He whistled, he sang, and he was very popular among the whole staff.

"He is too good to be true," I said to Johannes. He was always in such good humor, and his laughter and merriment were heard throughout the dining room. His gaiety spread over to the guests.

After a week I noticed that on Monday we had had fried chicken, on Tuesday roast beef, on Wednesday chicken, and on Thursday roast beef, on Friday chicken, and on Saturday roast beef. I was a little bit apprehensive about our menu since it was August and we had guests staying for three or four weeks at a time. I made a remark to Chef Joseph which made him flare up, saying that he didn't want to have women in the kitchen. The kitchen is a place for men, he said. Johannes begged me to keep away, so I did.

Another week passed and I finally had become really upset because the chicken-roast beef menu was still being adhered to. On that second Saturday I simply needed a change of atmosphere. I hopped in my little convertible, drove over to Burlington, and went from bookstore to bookstore looking for new releases, picking up some in each store to take home on consignment. Accumulating book packages as I went along, I finally felt really better and not nervous anymore, so I drove home.

As I drove up to the house, there was Johannes standing on the front steps dressed in his Sunday best. He came down and said, "Mother, can I help you with something?"

This was all very odd. I pointed at the few packages which I could have easily carried for myself. Johannes grabbed the packages and my elbow and steered me upstairs to my room. He closed the door and said, "Mother, sit down."

So I did, and Johannes solemnly announced, "Chef Joseph left together with the kitchen boy, one of our cars, and one of our helpers. I have notified the police. A roadblock has been arranged."

After a moment of deep silence I said, "Johannes, today is Saturday and the house is full. Did he at least have the roast beef in the oven?"

Johannes laughed out loud and said, "Yes, Mother, and the whole staff is helping to cut it and serve it."

At that moment the telephone rang. Johannes took the receiver and there was Chef Joseph's voice on the other end saying, "I needed the car to get me to the bus station in Burlington. The kitchen boy is coming with me, but the other boy is bringing the car back. And don't you try to find out anything because I gave you a false name and you will never find me." And he hung up.

He was right—we never heard from him again.

There were times of crises like this, with the house full of guests and no cook, when our staff rose to the occasion. Suddenly one of the waitresses said she knew how to make bread, another one knew how to make dessert, one of the boys had once worked in a restaurant and knew how to cut meat, and life went on without the guests ever suspecting the kitchen tragedy.

There were other tragedies—like when we were suddenly out of water. Not a drop of water was left when I in a desperate moment arranged a picnic near a waterfall, asking the guests to bring along their bathing suits for a swim (I really thought for a shower). And while I kept them there for a good three hours, the plumber outdid himself to repair the damage. When we came back, the water was flowing as usual.

"Mother, the ceiling in the dining room is dripping."

"Mother, it is pouring into the living room."

"Mother, bedroom No. 14 is wet already."

These were the battle cries in the middle of the winter when the ice had crawled up under the shingles and later started to melt. Suddenly, where you never expected it, it simply poured in a steady stream. These were the days when the kitchen was practically out of pots and pans because of the water "drippings." All the waiters and all the male employees were up on the roofs hacking away the ice. As much as we tried to forestall it, it happened every year.

It is absolutely unforeseeable what people might stuff into a toilet bowl only because they don't need it anymore. For instance, a pair of men's shorts, or a broken toy of a dear little one. Only after everyone was sitting at the dinner table would the water overflow first in the bathroom, and then into the adjoining living room, and finally appear outside in the hall. Then somebody would come down and say very nicely, "I think there is something wrong in Room 17."

Of course this would always be in the evening, and of course the plumber would just on that particular night have gone to the Rotary meeting, and of course his wife would hate to disturb him there, and so it would take quite some time before he would come with his equipment and finally produce the man's pants, the baby's toy, or what have you.

And you find yourself composing a sign for every bathroom:

"Please do not throw anything into. . . ."

Hours earlier we had assembled in my room to find out exactly when we had started the Trapp Family Lodge. Now after a lot of tears and laughter from reminiscing, somebody finally said, "What would you consider the highlight of the year, Mother?"

And without a moment's hesitation I said, "Christmas Eve."

Everybody agreed readily. We brought our own Christmas celebration across the Atlantic Ocean. Every year on the 24th of December, Johannes would go out into our own woods and cut a tall Balsam fir and bring it in still fragrant and fresh. For weeks before hand we had already started preparations: we wrapped candies in frilled tissue paper; we strung homemade cookies with red wool. They smelled fragrant, like gingerbread; we call it *Lebkuchen*. There were the meringue rings in different colors, and finally the glass balls and the old decorations like in the old home. When all this was hung on the tree, which was usually done by some of our girls, next came the silver chains, the silver hair, and at the very end our sixty candleholders with real wax candles in them.

Word had gotten around through the years, and the people came to the Trapp Family Lodge not so much for the skiing, but in order to see our Christmas tree with real candles. Then came the old ceremony. We would all assemble in the big living room across the courtyard, where I would tell a little bit about the Advent season and Christmas Eve as they are celebrated in Austria. I would explain that Austrian children have never seen or heard of Santa Claus. To them the Holy Child Himself comes and brings the tree and the gifts under it. Therefore, during the whole day of Christmas Eve the door of the living room was closed and everybody was tiptoeing around in order to not disturb the angels who were helping the Holy Child.

Finally, when it was getting dusk outside and everyone had reached the height of expectation, the sound of the silver bell could be heard. That meant only one thing—that the door of the living room would be opened again. And there it was—the big tree in its glory of the candlelight.

Every year it is touching how 120 or 150 grownups will quietly tiptoe in deep silence and, with some of the expectancy of their long-forgotten childhood, follow us across the long corridor to the open door with the big tree. They will all file in, and someone in the family will read "The Christmas Story." When he comes to the words, "And she wrapped Him in swaddling clothes and laid Him in a manger," the youngest of the children present—the littlest of all—will be given the figure of the Christ child and he will tiptoe over to the manger and put the Holy Child on the straw.

Then the gospel story is finished and we start singing "Silent Night," the first verse in German as it was sung that very first time in the little country church outside of Salzburg. The second verse is sung by everybody in English, and we always add one more verse in humming at the end while everybody is taking in the soft glow of the wax candles. Then everybody has to wish everybody else a blessed Christmas, and the packages under the tree are distributed to our help.

It became a tradition that whole families were coming to our Christmas celebration. Each child is allowed to take candy from the Christmas tree every day. At the end of the week the tree gets emptier and emptier, but the children's eyes—so full of Christmas expectancy—get shinier as the week goes on at the Trapp Family Lodge.

14

Interesting Friends

This Christmas I received a Christmas card again from the Bob Hope Family. After a very nice paragraph, it said, "Merry Christmas and a Very Happy New Year, from Dolores, Bob and the Family." Inside were pictures of the entire family. As I looked at it, fond memories came to me.

The very beginning goes back many, many years—more than twenty years it must be—when Dolores had a nursemaid for her children who were still pretty young. This girl had just read my book. Since she and Dolores were very much what we call practicing Catholics, she insisted that Mrs. Hope must go to the Trapp Family Lodge in Stowe, Vermont.

A telegram came with the reservation, and our secretary got all excited about it. I, never looking at TV and hardly ever reading a newspaper, wasn't hit that hard because I had no idea who Bob Hope was. But the whole household outside the family got happily apprehensive. When the big day came, a huge Chrysler station wagon arrived first with oodles and oodles of bags, suitcases, and every thinkable kind of luggage from the most elegant down to duffel bags. This about filled the lobby of the lodge. A little later another Chrysler arrived, out of which came Mrs. Bob Hope, her two girls and two boys, and tiny little Mimi, the nursemaid barely four feet high.

In no time we had merged into one happy family. They enjoyed everything we did, and they did it with us—beginning with mass in our chapel in the morning. They readily took to Austrian food which, of course, was homemade. At that time one of my older daughters was the cook. Anything we used to do in our family—like picnics, hikes, swims in mountain lakes—was enjoyed by all of us together.

The weeks passed incredibly fast and all of a sudden a telegram came saying that Bob Hope himself wanted to visit his family. How this became known to the Vermont newspapers I will never know. But as he arrived at the Montpelier Airport there were seventy-two press representatives. We have those tiny little papers in every town of 2,000 inhabitants, and each paper has its own reporter there.

Then even I, who hadn't thought of Bob Hope as being very important, was impressed. He didn't have much time, but the few hours he spent with all of us together were enough to show him at his most lovable best with that dry sense of humor which keeps you in a continuous uproar. Much later when I once saw him on TV, I thought, *If they would only let him be himself. He is so much more funny if you just leave him alone without so many props.*

It was quite a tearful farewell when the Bob Hope family left at the end of four weeks because their children and our children had become good friends, and Dolores and I were close friends by then too. We had to solemnly promise that whenever our concert tour took us to the West Coast we must visit them.

Half a year later on our return trip home from Hawaii we had three days off and were most joyfully received at the Bob Hope's. It happened to be Bob's fiftieth birthday, and everybody who is somebody in Hollywood came to a big party. I stood in a reception line next to Dolores. Since I hardly ever look at television, or listen to the radio, or read newspapers and magazines, and very seldom see a movie, my knowledge of show business people was restricted to Spencer Tracy (Father Flanagan in *Boys' Town,*) and Irene Dunne (*I Remember Mama*). Dolores had pity on me, so as she introduced everyone she would whisper after his name, "TV," or "stage," or "producer," etc.

But when one gentleman came, Dolores simply said, "Maria, this is Jack Benny."

I looked blank and said, "What is he doing?"

Dolores answered, "He's the nation's second-best comedian."

Whereupon I looked fisheyed and asked, "And who is the best?"

This turned into the best joke of the evening, and of course everybody thought it was staged.

I remember another thing about the Bob Hopes. During the last of our concertizing years we employed a New York publicity agent whom we paid thousands of dollars a year, every year. At the same time, we made it next to impossible for her to work with us because we didn't like to be photographed, we didn't care to have interviews, and we were rather embarrassed to see our pictures in the paper. Once as we departed from New York, heading again for the West Coast, our publicity lady took me aside and gave me a serious talking to.

"Look, Mrs. von Trapp, this is ridiculous. What are you paying me for if you don't provide me with material to write about? Every little episode that happens on the way, you telephone or telegraph to my office right away. Promise me."

And lamely I promised.

Nothing worth telling about happened until we arrived on the West Coast and stayed for two days at Bob Hope's. Bob was in Europe making a film, so Dolores put me in his room, which is next to hers, while the family stayed in the guest house. As she opened Bob's bedroom door, there was the largest, hugest bed I had ever seen. Just for the fun of it, I lay down on the edge of the bed and rolled across. It took me five "rollovers" to "reach the other shore." Then I sat in the middle and played with the buttons on the night table. I pushed button number one, and silently the big wardrobe door opened. Button number two, and the garage door opened. Before I finished with the buttons, I suddenly sat stock-still and cried out loud, "Dolores!"

As she came running from her room, I asked eagerly, "Please have a photographer take my picture for our publicity lady in New York—'Mrs. von Trapp in Bob Hope's bed.' "

Dolores smiled down at me and said, "Maria, I don't think you want this one."

After a moment I didn't think so either.

Even if our two very different lives and being 3,000 miles apart don't let us see much of each other, every time when I go out West for lectures, I stay with the Hopes. And whenever Dolores comes East, she tries to squeeze in a couple of days with us. It is a joy to realize each time that our visit is always just a continuation of our previous time together, as if we had only met last week.

Once more I was called to the West Coast for a series of lectures beginning in Los Angeles and going all the way to Seattle. Since my first lecture would be in Los Angeles, I called Dolores and asked whether she had time, in which case I would come a few days earlier. Then she could show me their new home in Palm Springs, which she had always wanted to do. It was just fine with her, so I left four days earlier and flew directly to Palm Springs. There I spent the most delightful days, with Dolores showing me around in this oasis in the middle of the desert, showing me the model of a new home to come while I enjoyed the one they lived in to the fullest. It was a Spanish-type house built around a patio, and the patio was practically filled with an Olympic-size swimming pool. I don't know who else ever uses it, but during the days I was there I practically lived in it, swimming being my passion.

Suddenly looking at a calendar across the room,

something occurred to me: For heaven's sake, today is the 31st of March, which means tomorrow is the first of April. And Bob Hope being Bob Hope—I'm not going to fall for any April Fool joke. So I asked Dolores, "Say, would it be possible for me to spend all day tomorrow in my room? I have a huge stack of unanswered mail with me, and I would very much like to get caught up."

"That suits me fine," Dolores said. "I have a few errands to run and a couple of visits. You'll get your meals in your room, Maria, and in the evening we will get together again."

And so it happened. Breakfast in my room and then the first swim. Then I honestly got out that stack of mail, sorted it in "musts" and "maybes" and then I began interrupting myself every so often with a vigorous swim across the large pool, sitting in the sunshine, continuing my correspondence.

At two o'clock in the afternoon the telephone rang. Immediately I perked up. *Ah ha!* I thought. *This is it.*

I took the phone and a voice said, "Mrs. Maria von Trapp, this is the White House calling."

"This is the Red House answering," I said coldly, because it so happened that Bob Hope's house was covered in red brick.

"But this really is the White House calling," the voice said.

"And this really is the Red House answering," I chuckled.

Now a rather exasperated voice said, "Mrs. von Trapp, whatever am I going to do with you? The President of the United States and the first lady request the honor of your company for April 10th. A state dinner is being given for the Chancellor of Austria, and you will be a guest of honor."

Inasmuch as it was her telephone bill, I was silent

for a dollar's worth. Then I meekly said, "Please don't mention what I have said to anybody."

A cheery voice answered, "I can hardly wait to hang up."

After I had solemnly agreed that I would be there, I tried to collect my thoughts. What I had expected to be an April Fool's joke instigated by Bob Hope had turned out to be a rather important invitation. I got dressed, put my mail away, and went in search of Dolores—who wasn't in. So I had to shelve my excitement for a little while. When she finally came in, I told her all about it.

After she had finished laughing, I said, "Dolores, what am I going to put on?"

I had told her that on April 10th I had to give a talk at one o'clock at an air force base outside St. Louis, and that I would be traveling until then on various lectures.

Dolores most kindly took me into her bedroom and, opening an immense wardrobe like at Sak's Fifth Avenue, showed me evening gowns in all materials and colors of the rainbow. But unfortunately, they were five sizes too small for me. (That was in the times before Weight Watchers.) I was really heartbroken because these were super-elegant gowns. One was all in gold and had trimming of something like very fluffy down. But what can you do if you are too big or they are too small?

But Dolores had a good idea. When she looked over my schedule, she saw that I had to stay overnight in Dallas, Texas, the day before going to St. Louis. In Dallas is the Neiman Marcus store, a place I remembered quite well because the year before I had given a talk there when they had their Austrian week in February. Dolores does a lot of shopping there, so she telephoned the man in charge of the dress department and explained the situation. Telling him that I would arrive late at night and would have to be at the airport at 12 noon the next day, she asked if he could take care of me in that amount of time. He assured her he could.

When I awoke in the morning at the Holiday Inn in Dallas, the telephone rang and a very nice and kind voice informed me that the big boss would be at my hotel at 9 o'clock. (Neiman Marcus opens its doors at 10, so we had one precious hour for ourselves.)

We whizzed through Dallas in a Cadillac convertible. When we arrived, three people were in attendance. One was in charge of dresses with three gowns to choose from; one was in charge of shoes, and one was in charge of the etceteras, like gloves, stockings and jewelry. Believe it or not, the first gown I laid my eyes on, I fell in love with at first sight; it was the one. Then it was easy to find the right shoes and other accessories, and the whole transaction hadn't even taken one hour. Everything was packed beautifully into one single big box, and the Cadillac convertible whizzed me to the airport.

I arrived in St. Louis, was met with an air force car by a colonel and his wife, and taken to the base. My lecture was at one o'clock, and the plane—the airfield was thirty miles away—left for Washington at three o'clock. I explained this tight situation to the colonel and a small airplane was very kindly put at my disposal after my talk. A most handsome young lieutenant was my pilot. Sitting next to him, I did a real foolish thing as we taxied on the runway, finding our way toward the TWA plane. Something just hit me, and I persuaded him to taxi right under the left wing of the jet in which I had to take off. I hope I didn't get him into trouble afterward; it was so funny—the small plane was like a chick under the wing of a mother hen.

Then I had to do one more piece of persuasion. I had to find my pilot of the TWA, for passengers were not allowed to take big luggage in front or in the passenger compartment. I, however, would have very little time after arriving in Washington, D.C., at 7:15 P.M., for I had to be at the White House at 8:00, including the driving from the airport to my friend's house where I would change. I had to make that clear to my pilot. After showing him the invitation to dinner at the White House, he really understood my plight and allowed my suitcase and big box from Neiman Marcus to be stored somewhere in the front of the plane.

Then everything went as fast as lightning. We arrived in Washington and I was allowed to be the first passenger out. My friend whizzed me in the height of traffic to her Arlington home where everybody helped me change and do my hair, and off we went to the White House.

This happened to be the week after the riots; the embers were still smoldering in the street which had had so many fires, and the curfew was still on. As I was absolutely certain I would be later than 10 o'clock in coming home I wondered how that would be handled. Then we were at the gate. I handed in my card, my name was called, and "my" lieutenant stepped forward and offered me his arm. I was genuinely glad to see him again.

I had been in the White House exactly a year before when our Senator Aiken, who had thought it was a shame that I never had been there, arranged an invitation for me for Armed Forces Day. That had really been something. It was my first visit to the White House and, as I arrived and showed my card, my name was called out loudly. A very handsome, tall, blond hair, blue-eyed young lieutenant stepped up and offered me his arm. He was to be my escort for the whole function.

I looked at him, full of compassion, and said, "I'm sorry I am not one of my daughters, but I'll try to make up."

Then we had a real ball together. We were like two young kids, he walking in my shadow. We simply enjoyed ourselves, going around and opening doors and peeking in; we saw much more of the White House than the rest of the guests did. Nobody stopped us and it was wonderful. Finally, when the waiting came to a close, he steered me to the East Room where all the other guests had assembled.

My goodness, what company I saw myself in. We had only generals and admirals in their finest dress uniforms, from all branches of the armed forces. As I am a navy wife, I singled out the navy of course. But I was stunned by the colorfulness of the marines. Not only the big shots, but also those in the marine band which was playing most of the time.

As there were so many guests there was not a reception line, but President Johnson and Lady Bird went from one little group to the other.

It was the beginning of May. In Vermont when I left it was in the mid-sixties. But Washington was already through with the cherry blossoms and it was a balmy day in the 80's.

Eventually the President and the first lady came to me also, and as he greeted me I thought I ought to tell him what I thought. So I said, "Mr. President, I am sorry, but I cannot agree with your policy in Vietnam."

He bent over me and said gently, "Mrs. von Trapp, you are not the only one," and they went on.

Then I turned to my escort and said, "It's awfully hot in here. Let's get out on the terrace."

There is one big wide terrace embracing the whole

East Wing and not a soul was there, so we enjoyed ourselves greatly, simply standing there and getting a little cooler air. Suddenly a general came practically running toward me, arms outstretched. Two steps behind him was his wife. He shook my hand and said, "I just heard that the real Maria from the *Sound of Music* is here, and my wife said she would never talk to me again if I wouldn't let her meet you."

That started something. One after the other came and it turned into a joint recital. While the President was going around inside, I held my private reception outside among all those two- three- four- and five-star generals with their ladies.

At each handshake I would turn toward my young escort and say, "General, may I introduce you to Lieutenant. . . ."

This way I tried to make up—as I had promised. He met all the big brass that day.

Suddenly there was in the distance a figure in civilian clothes also approaching me with his lady and his arms outstretched—War Secretary McNamara. We had a wonderful little chat and I thought, *This is a chance of a lifetime,* so I said, "Mr. Secretary, I have one great big tremendous request. I would so very much like to take the film, the *Sound of Music,* and go to Vietnam like Bob Hope does at Christmas. I would like to do it to entertain the soldiers and give them a little running commentary when the film is over. Could you help me get the permission?"

He said, "Write it down for me and send it over to my office in the Pentagon tomorrow. I'll do all I can."

He kept his promise. I was cleared by the CIS and the permission was granted. Unfortunately, only by the government—not by Twentieth Century Fox.

I was on cloud nine when suddenly I saw President Johnson and the first lady appear. They were wondering what was going on out on the porch. We shook hands once more with a big laugh, and that had been my first experience in the White House.

Now I was here again, and this was a happy meeting with "my" lieutenant, the same boy. It was so very tactful of whoever made the arrangements to pick out the boy who had come from Germany, spoke fluent German, and was in the American army. This time he did not stay with me; he only escorted me to the big hall where a number of guests were already waiting. But this time it was rather "a small number," about eighty. Each one of us was given the menu of the evening with a list of names of the guests present. It was arranged according to protocol, and since my name is in the *T*'s I happened to be the last one. There was only a quiet murmur to be heard, everybody speaking softly in expectancy of things to come, when suddenly the double door was thrown open. A major general appeared in colorful uniform, tapped the floor twice with his staff, and announced, "The President of the United States."

And a band struck the anthem. Even while I am telling it, it still goes cold down my spine. This is always a great moment.

Then he announced again: "The Chancellor of Austria, Dr. Klaus."

And the Austrian anthem was heard. The two couples were standing now in a reception line, and we began to file past them. I had known Dr. Klaus for many, many years when he had been governor in Salzburg. We were quite good friends, but obviously tonight I wasn't supposed to show that. When it was my turn to greet the President of the United States, who would believe my astonishment when Mr. Johnson bent over me again and said, "And now, Mrs. von Trapp?"

This was exactly a week after he had stepped down, declaring he would not run again, and had begun to take our troops out of Vietnam. I was really touched.

I looked up, took his hand with both of mine, and said, "I admire you, Mr. President."

Then I said a very formal "Good evening" to my old friend, Dr. Klaus, and I thought the kissing I must save for later.

Then out of nowhere my young lieutenant appeared to escort me to the dining room. There we sat at tables of eight and I happened to be seated with one of the daughters of President Johnson and her husband. This was wonderful because I heard many little human-interest stories of her mother and father. When dinner was over we stood around in small groups, balancing small coffee cups or liqueur glasses, when suddenly President Johnson crossed the room, heading for me. He took me by the elbow and we went over to Dr. Klaus. I could feel that I had been the big surprise which he wanted to exhibit.

"Here is somebody special," he said to Dr. Klaus. "A former countryman of yours, and now our pride and joy, the real Maria from the *Sound of Music*, Mrs. von Trapp."

Dr. Klaus and I managed somehow to keep a straight face and act astonished, but a little later we met behind one of those decorated palm trees in the big room and exchanged memories from Salzburg.

However, what I took home from that evening as the most outstanding memory was the fact that President Johnson, who most certainly must have met thousands of people within that year, many of whom might not have agreed with his Vietnam policy, should have remembered what I had said. I couldn't believe it!

15

The Gift Shop

Through our many travels crisscrossing all over America, it had become known that our headquarters was in Stowe, Vermont. As a result, many people who visited New England made a little extra side trip to see the Trapp Family Singers in their home. Each time after such a visit somebody would say with embarrassment, "Do you mind very much if I ask for your autograph?"

Suddenly it hit me: If these people were able, for instance, to buy postal cards of our house or of the family, they wouldn't be half so embarrassed to ask for an autograph. When I mentioned this around the family table one evening, it was met with stunned silence.

In the very same week we had to go to Maine to visit friends there, and on the way we saw a big sign on a huge wooden barn: "Swedish Handicrafts." We stopped the car and walked in.

It was a beautiful gift shop with Swedish cut glass, ceramics, metal work and other works of art. We made a few purchases and, as I paid, I asked the lady, "Where in the world do you get these beautiful things?"

"At 225 Fifth Avenue," she answered.

I was too embarrassed to ask more questions, so I

repeated to myself, "225 Fifth Avenue, 225 Fifth Avenue," and finally wrote it down in the car.

After our short visit in Maine, we returned on another route. And there it happened again: My eye was caught by a huge sign, "Gift Shop." We stopped the car, and this time we saw beautiful things from Mexico, China, Japan and India. We bought a few little things and I asked, "Where in the world do you find such beautiful gifts?"

And, lo and behold, the laconic answer was: "At 225 Fifth Avenue."

This time I said, "Please, may I ask what is there?"

And a friendly saleslady explained that it was a wholesale house in New York City with gifts from all over the world, where people who run a gift shop go shopping.

The lady cautioned me, however, "This place is only for wholesalers; no one else can buy there."

Unknowingly she had nipped in the bud my fervent wish to go and do my Christmas shopping at 225 Fifth Avenue. I realized if I wanted to do that I would have to have a gift shop.

And why not? What does one need for a gift shop? First, a room. I went around the house in search of the room. Right next to our living room was our music room with the piano and our vast music library. How about this one? Yes, it would do.

Second, one needed money to buy things at 225 Fifth Avenue in order to sell them at home. I had privately saved $500, so one evening I came out boldly with the announcement that I wanted to start our own gift shop—if possible, with objects from Austria. I explained to the family members who had not been in the car on the trip to Maine about the many things I had seen in the Swedish and Oriental gift shops.

The family was rather aloof, but Father Wasner was

loudly and distinctly against it. And he remained so, even as he took me to the airport to go to New York on my first pilgrimage to 225 Fifth Avenue. This was the only time that I did something absolutely against his outspoken wish and command.

I was so sure that if I could buy something for five dollars and sell it for ten dollars, even if I counted expenses, there had to be a little profit. And for once in my life I was right when it came to business.

I didn't understand Father Wasner's misgivings. However, I did understand the careful silence of my grownup children because, so far, I had shown clearly and distinctly that I had no head whatsoever for business. I must say that I astonished even myself when this gift shop blossomed forth from a one-room homemade affair in the house to a separate building situated half a mile down the road from the lodge.

I still remember vividly how I hailed a taxi and said, "225 Fifth Avenue, please."

I was really and truly excited as I stepped into the building which had formerly been a hotel and was now one of the headquarters for the gift business in New York. Downstairs I was asked whether I had a gift shop, where it was located, and what was its name.

Name—what *was* its name? On the spur of the moment I invented the Trapp Family Gift Shop in Stowe, Vermont. And so it remains to this day.

Then I walked on clouds and never came down. It was like one huge big Christmas Eve. Gifts from all countries of the globe, in all prices and sizes, made of ceramics, porcelain, glass, paper, wood, metal, etc., etc., etc. A very nice lady in the lounge downstairs had informed me that on the seventh floor was a buyer's lounge and if I had any questions whatsoever, this was the place to go and ask.

So I made my way to the buyer's lounge after a

while and investigated where I could find gifts from Austria. This was in 1951 and my accent must have still been quite pronounced, but I had discovered that Americans didn't mind accents; in fact, they like them. They are most willing to help you. So I was told where to find Austrian gifts.

On the way there I saw the words "Swedish Imports," and in I went.

There stood Mrs. Idlene Lane, a lovely Swedish saleslady who that very morning had opened her booth. I was her first customer, and she was my first adventure in wholesale buying. So I was handed from one shop to the next and I was wallowing in Austrian wood carvings, ceramics, embroidery, and wrought-iron works.

Of course, there was a question of money. In order to get as much as possible, I tried to keep the retail price between one and five dollars.

I spent two deliriously happy days at 225 Fifth Avenue from 9:00 in the morning until they closed at 5:30 P.M. I doubt that a person in her right mind would go to a museum for that length of time. But while going to a museum only entails looking, going shopping in a wholesale gift show means looking and deciding. Yes or no, and how much? I have found out time and time again in my life that if one enjoys his work, he is not easily tired out. So on my third day I returned home, triumph on my face. I couldn't wait for the things to arrive.

Within two weeks, with the help of my family, the two rooms were turned into "The Trapp Family Gift Shop." In one room we had also put four tables where we sold coffee, hot chocolate and *Linzertorte*—a typical Austrian pastry made of nuts and almonds which keeps forever. It was all very much homemade. The girl who was our secretary in the front office also took care of the gift shop if we were not at home. Book-keeping was very simple, just writing down the purchases in one big book.

This went on for a few years. In the meantime I had learned that, besides 225 Fifth Avenue, there is the New York Gift Show in the Coliseum with an immense display of gifts from literally all over the world. So every February and August I do most of my shopping there.

One day it happened that I wanted a special music box which could play "Silent Night," and the man from whom I had bought it for years said to me, "I am sorry but I am out of it, but next week I am going to the Frankfurter Messe and there I will get the newest patterns and I will get you some."

Out of sheer mischief, I said playfully, "And why can't I go myself to the Frankfurter Messe and pick it up?" Not meaning a word of it.

The effect, the impact, of my words was astounding. The man got very excited and, throwing up his hands, he said, "For heaven's sake, what an idea! *You* can't go to the Frankfurter Messe. Only wholesalers like us may do that. You would buy a whole railroad car full of every item!"

Well, that sounded a little exaggerated to me, but I still was only teasing when I made the same remark in a few other places, receiving the same excited reaction, with the same exclamation: "You can't go; only we can."

And I said it once more to an elderly gentleman from whom I had bought all those years.

He said quietly, "I have wondered for years why you didn't go."

Of course, he didn't let on as to why he never advised me to go, but at least he was all for it.

"There is only one piece of advice I'll give you," he

175

said. "Get yourself a letter of credit from your bank to a bank in Frankfurt, as this will be your first time there and they do not know you."

When I came home I realized I had only five days' time to get ready. I caused a little uproar in our local bank, which had to quickly telegraph and telephone to make arrangements, but finally $10,000 was deposited in the Bank of New York in Frankfurt.

In the meantime, the gift shop had outgrown the two rooms in the main house and was transferred down the road where it is now ten times the original size, with a big warehouse underneath. The four tables where we served coffee and cake ended up as a Viennese Kaffee Haus with a big porch where people can sit in the open in the summer months. The menu has also grown from coffee and cake into many different Austrian specialties.

My first visit to the Frankfurter Messe was just a repetition of my excitement the first time I went to 225 Fifth Avenue, except that this time there was a whole big fairground with many buildings. I tried to find out which building contained handicrafts, but the whole thing was ten times as big as the New York Fair and I had to learn to find my way around.

The great excitement of the first day occurred after my first purchase, which happened to be in the line of ceramics, when a German gentleman asked my name. I said, "Trapp Family Gift Shop in Stowe, Vermont, and I am Mrs. Maria von Trapp."

He dropped the pencil with which he was writing, grabbed my hand with both of his, and said, "Oh, I am so happy to meet you personally. I have seen your film, I have read your book, I must tell my wife!"

No words were asked about a letter of credit, and this went on from place to place throughout the whole fair. I had paid twenty dollars to have the money sent to Frankfurt, and later paid twenty dollars again to have it sent back to America—unused. It was a wonderful feeling that everybody seemed to know us and like us and trust us.

The misgivings and suspicions from the cautious members of the family and Father Wasner had long since disappeared. The Gift Shop is doing fine.

Of course, I have found out that I could make at least ten times as much money if I had a souvenir shop with items like the Statue of Liberty, from the size of a thimble to the size of a large container for umbrellas, or the greatest best seller of two years ago, or a toilet-seat ashtray with the wording "Trapp Family Gift Shop, Stowe, Vermont," printed on the outside. But from the very beginning I decided that the shop would be a wonderful opportunity to give beauty a chance, so I only hand-pick things which strike me as beautiful and perfect in their realm.

Since this first beginning in Frankfurt, I have gone every year—sometimes even twice—to different international gift shows in Europe. There is the Wiener Messe which takes me to Vienna, there is one in Innsbruck, one in Salzburg, one in Graz, and during these visits I have become acquainted with young artists, especialy wood-carvers. It has become an altogether delightful business; not only must I go to Europe every year—a wonderful thing for me—but I also help young artists on their hard road to fame and fortune.

Many of our guests have told me a great many times what a pleasure it is for them to browse among all those truly beautiful things, and many do their Christmas shopping in the summer. Numerous items are purchased during the year for wedding presents and birthday gifts, etc.

In the meantime we have discovered how to have

postal cards made, and you can imagine how astounded I was myself when I recently asked our dear saleslady, Louise, "How many picture cards of me do you usually sell in one year?"

"Between thirty and forty thousand," she replied.

Of course, like everything I have learned in my life, I also learned the gift shop business the hard way. After all these years, I am still making major mistakes at the twentieth year of its existence.

Louise had told me a year ago that I had bought too few calenders. Louise is the manager of the gift shop, my right-hand girl, and she keeps things going and in order. They were those picture calendars with wonderful colored photographs of Austria, the Alps, the Dolomites, Italy, Alpine flowers, or people in different Alpine costumes, etc. So when I went over in 1970 I selected from all of those beautiful calendars without watching how many I was ordering.

When I returned home and gave Louise my purchase orders, she added them up on her adding machine and suddenly gave me a strange look.

"Mother, do you know how many calendars you bought?"

"No, I don't, but I hope this time it will be enough," I answered, remembering her constant reprimand of the previous year.

She said laconically, "2,220."

That worked like a shot. I realized that if I had bought too many wood carvings, or too many cups and saucers, they could be sold throughout the years, whereas a calendar has 1972 mercilessly printed outside and has to be sold in that time.

I made it my business to sell those calendars. This last summer I practically lived in the gift shop, and every so often I would approach nice-looking people and say, "Would you do me a favor, please?"

They always most heartily assured me they would. And I would say, "Please buy a calendar. I bought too many."

They laughed and always obliged, and by the end of the season, the last calendar was gone.

16

A Late Vocation

Here I am living in the ski country. "There is always snow in Stowe, you know" is the old slogan. So from the very first days when we took guests into our home, there were skiers in the winter. And for many an endless winter I had to sit through dinners listening to how the snow was on this or that trail. For instance, while it was all right on the Standard, the Nose Dive was miserable. So Mr. Jones and his wife finally had to retreat to the Spruce Peak. Tomorrow morning they will start out on Lullabye Lane. By and by I knew all the slopes' names and they were like real cousins to me, except I myself was still not on skis.

While I was in school in Vienna the skiing had been only for the very rich—to whom I didn't belong. My two years in Nonnberg are self-explanatory as to why I didn't make any progress in skiing then.

As soon as I was married, the three younger children contracted scarlet fever and I nursed them at home. They were barely well when I started having fever and getting red all over. Of course, I took it for granted that now it was my turn with the scarlet fever. But the doctor, for some unknown reason, didn't believe so. He said it was only the small measles, not the German measles. I didn't have to lie in bed; it would be over in a few days. He proved to be wrong when I finally started to scale all over my body. Then he had to admit that it had been scarlet fever. Unfortunately, because of no bed rest and no care, I developed kidney trouble. This interferred greatly with my having babies. Among the eight children God sent me, only three remained alive. That involved many years when, again, I didn't feel like going skiing.

But then the time came when I felt perfectly fine. I got a little bit impatient listening to all that ski talk. So, for my forty-fifth birthday I asked for only one thing—a complete outfit for skiing. And I got it.

In Austria you celebrate a birthday the night before, so the lucky birthday child has a whole day of twenty-four hours ahead of him where he is the number one person and has all kinds of little wishes granted. So on the evening before the 26th of January, there was my table covered with brand-new warm Olympic underwear, ski pants, a couple of pullovers, a windbreaker and, last but not least, a pair of skis with bindings, and next to them the boots. I looked at all of this tenderly; in the eye of my mind, with the help of my proverbial imagination, I saw myself sweeping down Mount Mansfield.

Next morning Johannes, age nine, said most eagerly, "Mother, there is nothing to it. Come with me. I'll show you."

He helped me put on my skis. I hobbled across the courtyard and across the street, and right there I took off after Johannes. A meadow there slopes very, very gently toward the woods in the valley. There really didn't seem to be anything much to skiing. My skis followed in Johannes' tracks, and I felt on top of the world.

Why the little boy had to go all the way down, I don't know, and why was he heading toward the woods, I didn't understand. But he was. Single trees were growing in the meadow, and I did what everybody else does when he learns to ride a bicycle. If he wants to avoid a post still far away, he will focus on it until he surely hits it. This is what I did with a young spruce tree maybe twelve feet high.

How I wanted to avoid the tree! But suddenly it bent under me between my two skis when I hit it with all my weight. The tree went up, and I sat straddling it, with my legs dangling down on either side. Johannes was standing underneath, doubled up with laughter. I could have squeezed the daylights out of him.

"Get me down!" I shouted.

There was the little boy shaking his mother from the tree like a ripe plum. Down came my skis, and I walked home on foot, deciding *never*, but *never*, to learn to ski with a member of my family.

So—what to do next? I was determined to learn how to ski.

We're lucky. We live only six miles from the tallest mountain in Vermont where Sepp Ruschp, a countryman of ours from Austria, has started several of the greatest, biggest, and best ski schools in the East. Therefore, Stowe is called the ski capital of the East. I decided to go there to the ski school. They had beginners' classes, and I was assigned to one with seven young kids. I was pupil number eight. The teacher took us up a very gentle slope and then showed us how to come down in a maneuver called a snowplow. This I could do, and again I felt like a million dollars. The next thing he tried was to make us do little turns —snowplow turns. After great trouble and getting mixed up with both of my feet, I finally succeeded in doing that too. Then the teacher instructed us to ski down and, just before we reached him, to do a certain something which would make us stop. But I simply couldn't learn that certain something. Five times, six times, seven times I had gone up, and each time I came down—shooting directly at him and landing around his neck. Finally I said, "Let me try once more."

As I walked up I thought, *If it doesn't work this time I might not ever learn it.*

As I was standing up there, the instructor whispered across the slope, "Mrs. von Trapp, you have to do it with your fanny."

Now, I had never heard that word used in that connection. For me, it was a girl's name with a capital *F,* and I thought he meant my youngest daughter.

So I stage whispered right back, "We don't have a Fanny in our family." I assumed he wanted me to practice with her.

That became the joke of the season. Whenever I came into the cafeteria, sooner or later I heard that nice little word mentioned by someone.

By the way, I did not learn how to stop like that on my skis. In the meantime, the course was over and, a little bit ashamed, I went home with my snowplow turn. That was all I could achieve for the time being.

Then some years passed and, with sickness on my part or sickness in the family, somehow or another I didn't get my skis out for quite a number of winters. Not until I got frisky again and started to practice my snowplow turn on the Toll House slope, which is right under Mount Mansfield.

This time I went with Johannes, who by that time had graduated from high school and had become a student at Dartmouth College. In the winter he was a ski instructor there. So I asked if he would come on one Sunday afternoon and help me learn the next step after a snowplow turn. He gladly agreed.

As we came down a couple of times on the practice slope, Johannes exclaimed, "Oh, Mother, you are really very good! Let's go up the Toll Road."

186

Was I flattered! We went up the big chair lift. Johannes set me straight, with my face down, and simply said, "Follow me."

I did. The Toll Road is our longest trail, four miles long and really most enjoyable. Never very steep. You don't have to know too much to come down on it and enjoy it. Unfortunately, I obviously was not quite ready yet. It was Sunday afternoon toward the end of the season, and great big moguls had been built up which the skier had to know how to cope with. Moguls are round mounds of snow which form on every slope when the same spot is hit by a few hundred skis. A skier either learns to go around them or, if he is good enough, ski over them. I couldn't go around them or over them so, with a terrible crash, I fell. Suffering a most piercing pain, I cried out loud.

Johannes, who had already disappeared a few hundred feet below, came running up on his skis and said, "Oh, no, Mother, not again! What have you broken this time?" He was referring to a few breaks I had experienced before—in my left arm, right arm, left foot and right foot. So, lying on my back, he had me wiggle my foot and then wiggle my arms. Neither one hurt, so he said consolingly, "Oh, Mother, you will have a most awful bruise tomorrow; you will radiate in all colors of the rainbow. But now, pick up your skis and let's go down."

At that moment the ski patrol arrived with a toboggan and volunteered to take me down on that. But Johannes, the strict teacher, said, "No, if she doesn't continue on skis now she may never touch them again."

And so, lovingly but sternly, he said, "Go on, Mother."

So I missed the only toboggan ride I have ever been offered in my life.

Well, I went down—but with no pleasure. I fell four or five times, and each time the scrambling up was getting more tiresome and more painful. *I must have an awful bruise,* I thought, *because my back aches like the dickens.*

Johannes had shot ahead of me and was waiting for me down below. When I reached him, I said, "Johannes, I hope you don't mind if you go on skiing alone. I think I'll nurse my bruise. My back aches so much."

Johannes said he understood fully, and he helped me take my skis off, put them in my car, and I was on the way back. I thought that just in order to make sure, I'd ask the doctor, who has his office on the Mountain Road, to check me over. The good doctor, who nurses about seven hundred breaks in one winter season, put me before the X ray, and I showed him where I ached.

He confirmed Johannes' statement; it would be a tremendous bruise. He couldn't see any breaks, but he said, "Why don't you come over to the hospital tonight, and tomorrow I'll take a complete X ray of your back. If you will come tonight, I will take you as my first patient tomorrow morning."

That made sense. I went home, got my toothbrush, nightgown, and a couple of books, and checked into the hospital in our neighboring town of Morrisville, where I had the run of the hospital. I went around visiting patients and nurses, and finally I went to bed with my aching back. The next morning I was patient number one in the X-ray room. I still remember how I hoisted myself onto the table and stretched out. After a few minutes the door opened.

In came Dr. Bryan, who pronounced solemnly, "Don't move. You have a broken back."

It gave me the shivers to think that with the broken vertebra I had skied down the whole long Toll Road, fallen, gotten up four or five times, ran up and down the stairs at home, and hoisted myself onto the X-ray table. Suddenly I wasn't supposed to move a finger.

I asked to be transferred to the University Hospital, at Burlington, where a dear friend, a university professor, put me in a plaster cast extending from my chin to my big toe. I was supposed to remain in it for at least half a year.

Our very best friend in this country also happened to be a university professor at Burlington. A research heart specialist, he was quite upset about me lying like a mummy in this plaster tomb. One of his friends happened to be President Kennedy's doctor, Dr. Kraus, whom the President used as his personal specialist for his back trouble. Dr. Kraus didn't believe in plaster of paris. He never put a broken limb in plaster, only in a splint. When Dr. Raab, our friend, mentioned my condition to Dr. Kraus, he threw up his arms and said, "For heaven's sake, bring her down."

They almost needed a crane to get me on the plane, and my poor doctor had great misgivings about what was going to happen to me. In New York my tremendous cast was peeled off me. Although I had only been in it three weeks, I already felt weak and helpless and simply didn't want to stand up straight. Dr. Kraus was very firm and said there were no two ways about it—either I did what he said or I went home. So I did what he said—with tears streaming down my face for days in a row. But, oh, what a miracle! In ten days I was completely healed and didn't have the slightest pain anymore; I came home on the airplane all by myself—as good as new. But, somehow or another, my eagerness to learn to ski had abated, and years passed.

Then came the glorious winter when Johannes, who had already taken over the management of the Trapp Family Lodge, started a completely new program in skiing—cross-country skiing.* Cross-country skiing was next to unknown. It had been tried here and there in Vermont, but never on a big scale. Johannes had the vision that the future of skiing was there, so he started with one Norwegian ski teacher, a tiny little workshop built into our garage, and about fifty pairs of rental skis and shoes in all sizes. Then on a very small scale, he advertised. And—lo and behold—the people came from all sides! At the end of the season he had five hundred people skiing on the trail he had laid out the previous fall with his Norwegian ski instructor friend, Per Soerli.

Right after Christmas I joined the ranks. A little timidly at first, but then with growing confidence, I went on "Highway No. 1"—as I called it—as far as to the point where the trail turns steeply up. This is where I didn't turn up but back. After having done this a number of times and for a number of days, I got frisky again. One day I hopped in the car and went over to Mount Mansfield where Sepp Ruschp, our famous Austrian countryman, had his office.

I walked in and said, "Sepp, among the eighty ski instructors, would you have one single one who would have enough patience for an elderly lady with two left feet?"

He smiled, did a moment of thinking, and said, "Yes, I have exactly the man for you—Pepi Gabl."

Arrangements were made for me to meet Pepi Gabl at 12 noon the next day at Spruce Peak.

Pepi Gabl had been an Olympic skier in Austria and, in that particular year, his young daughter Gertrude earned a gold medal at the Olympics. Skiing skill really ran in their family; but much more, Pepi

---

* See the article on cross-country skiing in the Jan. 14, 1972, issue of *Life* magazine.

was a teacher by the grace of God. You cannot become a teacher because you say so. A teacher is God-made, not man-made. Pepi was one of those.

With very few words, he showed me a little bit at a time. The way he looked at me, the way he encouraged me, he infused the wish and finally the know-how, so that in no time I did it after him. Pepi became my idol. The first day he did only snowplow turns, and out of my past came a little knowledge. Fortified with Pepi's confidence and nice glowing exclamations, I really and truly felt on top of the world this time.

After my first lesson with Pepi I was so full of enthusiasm and gratitude that on the way home I stopped at Sepp's office and walked right in, grabbed him around the neck, squeezed him, and said, "Sepp, I can't thank you enough for giving me Pepi Gabl."

He took one look at me, held me at arm's length, and said sternly, "Maria, you need new ski pants. Look at yourself."

It had completely escaped my attention that almost twenty years had passed since I had gotten my first ski-pants. The fashions had turned to stretchables, whereas I was looking a little bit like Winnie the Pooh on skis with the wind flapping my pants when I came down the slopes. Well, that was a little anticlimax to my enthusiasm. But trying to oblige, I went from one ski shop to another in Stowe. There are six of them, but not one—sorry to say—had my size. So I had to continue in my Winnie the Pooh pants—except now I was conscious of it.

It would give me the greatest pleasure to describe every single lesson minutely because it was such clear joy, but suffice it to say that two weeks after my sixty-fourth birthday, I came down Lullabye Lane on Mount Mansfield, the big mountain, behind Pepi Gabl.

Every spring for years and years, Johannes had mentioned, "Mother, it would be so good if we could have a few riding horses. The guests would so enjoy it!"

I don't know why I was so hard of hearing. But I was worried that the guests might have accidents, and I simply couldn't quite see it. So I always evaded the issue.

Another spring came, and Johannes had become a little impatient.

"Mother, how would it be if you would go down to Stowe? There is that little riding school now with those very nice tame horses. Just try taking a ride on horseback—just walking through the woods. I tell you, it's beautiful."

So Johannes' mother listened to her son's advice. And once she was on the back of a horse, you could hardly get her down anymore. Not only did I think it was beautiful to walk through the woods on horseback; I was most eager now to get horses for the Trapp Family Lodge. I did not notice that this was exactly what Johannes had been hoping for. He didn't show his enthusiasm outwardly. Very matter of factly he went about it, and in no time we had accumulated twelve riding horses. Everybody was happy—most of all myself.

But let it be said here, as both advice and a warning: Go step by step, and not two steps at once. I simply couldn't wait to know enough about riding. I liked galloping so much that twice I woke up in the hospital. Each time the horse on which I was sitting had changed its mind without telling me and made a right-angle turn while I continued to go straight ahead.

Once when I woke up in the hospital a doctor was bent over me. He informed me that I had broken all twelve ribs. I must have looked a little incredulous because he said, "You don't believe it? Look." And then he practically played a piano with my ribs, pushing each one down a little bit for me to see.

Now, there is absolutely no danger around broken ribs, so I got very little compassion and sympathy. No alarm is seen in any of the faces around you, but I assure everybody—it hurts like sin. You can't laugh, you can't sneeze, you can't blow your nose, you can barely breathe, and you breathe shallowly. If someone should accidently touch your bed, you could scream. It takes weeks and weeks to heal. At least it made me a little more cautious. It made me take enough riding lessons until I was finally able to stay on a horse, even if he should change his mind regarding directions.

But to go on a long ride through the woods, either in the spring or in the fall when the whole Vermont countryside turns into a symphony of colors, I cannot recommend it highly enough.

When people come and say with a small laugh, "What, me on skis? I have never been on skis, and I'm past thirty now," it just makes me laugh and I tell my story. The same thing happens when somebody informs me that he has never been on a horse and that he is over forty.

There are times when it comes in handy when I can inform everybody that even a late vocation, like mine, will give the utmost joy and pleasure.

17

Joyful Serving

In recent years I have made somewhat of a name for myself as a lecturer. Because of the number of requests that come in, I seldom pay much attention to the details except to note the date. Therefore, the request for an address to be given in a small town in Rhode Island might have been given scant attention except for the subject. They wanted me to speak on the topic, "How to serve the Lord joyfully."

I liked the topic, and I liked the idea of going to Rhode Island because it happens to be the state where two of my married children live and where I have six grandchildren in one family and seven in another.

So at the drop of a hat I agreed to go to Rhode Island. But I cannot describe my horror when I later discovered what was expected of me.

When I arrived in Rhode Island I called the church to ask how long they expected me to speak, how many people they expected to be present, and what kind of an audience it would be—a family group, youngsters or adults. In reply I was told that my talk would be the sermon at the Sunday morning mass in a Catholic church at the 10:30 A.M. service.

Now, I am a loyal church member, and I have known church protocol from my early days as a postulant in a convent in Salzburg, Austria. Of course, this simply couldn't be. Immediately I said, "I am a woman. I don't think I am allowed to talk in church, let alone give a sermon. I must ask my bishop."

So I picked up the telephone. But my bishop in Burlington, Vermont, was sick and couldn't answer. His assistant was very doubtful about the whole matter.

"If I were you, I wouldn't do it," he said.

"Father, I am very doubtful about it myself, and I don't want to do it; but I must have a strict order. My not wanting to do it isn't enough. Can't you forbid it?"

"No," he said, "unfortunately, this I can't do."

I banged down the telephone and turned to the local priest.

"How about your bishop? Have you asked him?"

"Sorry, he died two weeks ago."

For the next twenty-four hours I was reduced to mental pulp. I simply couldn't think. Not one idea came to me about what I could say on the subject, "How to serve the Lord joyfully."

Around and around I went in mental circles—physical also. I went for a hike along the beach. I sat around moaning and groaning in the house of my daughter. Finally I grabbed a Bible and disappeared under the trees in the garden. Desperately I turned pages, hardly reading anything. That night I slept poorly, waking up continually.

Morning finally came. Somehow I got through breakfast and when at 10:30 we marched out of the vestry in the rear of the large church I felt like a lamb being led to the slaughter. A group of altar boys headed the procession, and two readers followed. Sandwiched between the readers and two priests was little me. I had to go all the way up into the sanctuary. There I was motioned to a seat, and holy mass began.

If you were to take a big grain bag, empty it completely, and shake it good, and then look inside, you would know how empty I felt. But after the gospel was read, the priest introduced me and motioned me to step forward.

All I could manage to do was quietly whisper, "Dear Holy Spirit, *You* say it. Here are my lips."

Then—in complete astonishment—I listened to a most marvelous account of how we cannot serve the Lord joyfully without special help from the Holy Spirit. By listening, I learned that the apostles weren't able to do it either. They had gone through three years of public life with their best Friend and Savior day and night, really learning to know Him. Then they had gone through those three terrible days, and most of them had run away in fright. They witnessed His resurrection, but still didn't understand. They couldn't believe it. Up to the last hours of His forty days on earth they didn't quite know how to take Him. Every time He appeared He had to start over again with them by saying, "Fear not, it is I." They most certainly were not serving Him joyfully.

Finally, when He led them up to the Mount of Olives, He gave them a few last instructions: "It is so necessary for you that I go now to the Father because I will send you the One who will make you understand everything. You go back to Jerusalem now, and there you must wait for Him and pray for Him." They obeyed and for nine days and nine nights they stayed together, asking and praying for the Comforter, the Paraclete, the One to come whom Jesus had spoken of. They didn't know exactly what they were praying for, but He had told them to do so. And after nine days were over, He came.

What happened then? The door was thrown open and out they came—120 excited, exuberant, joyful people.

It had never occurred to me before that morning

what must have gone on to attract the sober bystanders who came running. Did they hear the noise of the wind? Did they see the tongues of flame? Why did they say, "They are drunk!"

These people who were filled with the Holy Spirit must have behaved in the fullness of joy—just as we do when we welcome a long-absent loved one at the airport. After the time of waiting, there is much embracing and kissing and shouting for joy. I think this is exactly what was going on. These people were in each other's arms saying, "Praise the Lord! Praise the Lord!" even as do the last five psalms. Now for the first time they were rejoicing in the Lord.

As I continued to listen to my sermon, in amazement I heard myself say, "We Catholics really go strong during Lent. No cake. No candy. No drinks. No smokes. Wonderful! For forty solemn days we are intense, long-faced—meaning every bit of it.

"Then comes Easter Sunday. What an anticlimax. Now we don't have anything more to do. He is risen. He doesn't need our sacrifices, and we really don't know what to do with Him. But we haven't learned yet to go the way of joyful resurrection with Him. We honestly and truly haven't learned to rejoice in the Lord or to serve Him joyfully.

"There is only one remedy. We must go into our upper room and take our Lord at His word: 'Go and wait for His coming.' And if we do, He surely will send that very same Comforter, the One who will explain everything to us. Only then, and only from then on, will we be able to be really joyful in the Lord."

My sermon ended there. Then, against all custom and practice in a Catholic church, the entire congregation broke out into applause. And, oh horror, I found myself applauding also, because I had listened to that sermon myself. After one clap I had my hands behind the pulpit, hoping that nobody had noticed.

Holy mass proceeded, and at the conclusion the priest stepped up to the microphone.

"Those of you who wish to remain and ask the baroness questions may do so. The rest of you are dismissed."

But only a few left. And again, I wondered to myself, *What will He say now?*

A number of questions were asked, and I gave answers. Then a woman raised her hand, but I couldn't understand what she was saying. So I asked her to repeat the question. She did, but I still didn't get it. So I invited her to come forward and speak into the mike so all could hear her question. She did, but she made the mistake of clutching the microphone in her hand and shouting into it. The rafters reverberated, the windows shook, but I couldn't understand a single word.

I was too embarrassed by that time to ask her to repeat her question another time. And I was on the spot; I had to answer.

Again I just had time to say, "Dear Holy Spirit, please answer."

And then I listened to myself say, "In such cases we simply fall back on what our Lord must have meant when He said, 'Happy are you if you are poor. And lucky are you if you hunger and thirst. And congratulations to you if they kick you around and you don't find justice down here, because your reward will be great in heaven.' The poor and the destitute will readily understand that, and it might even make them smile."

The lady obviously was satisfied, but I could hardly wait to get over to the rectory to find out what question she had asked. There I learned from the priest that she was a social worker, dealing with the poorest of the poor, the very destitute. Her question was: "How can I ask them to rejoice in the Lord if they don't have enough to eat, nothing to put on, and perhaps no job?" Surely the Holy Spirit had given a fitting answer.

After a joyful breakfast in the rectory, I sneaked back into the church and, with a heart bursting with thanks, told the Lord that from then on I would take Him even more at His word because that day He had shown me clearly that, upon my asking, He had sent the Holy Spirit to help.

18

Sound of Music

When my first book appeared in 1949 it didn't set the world on fire. As one reviewier said later, "The book has one mistake, the wrong title."

For that reason *The Story of the Trapp Family Singers* was placed in the music section of the bookstores and the libraries, and it took many years for the people to catch on that it was our life story.

Once there came a little stir from Hollywood when one of the film companies wanted to buy the book. But they immediately said, "We buy only the title; we make our own story to fit it."

This I couldn't do, so I had to give up the fame of Hollywood.

Years passed. The book had been translated into different languages, including German. In Germany it made a much greater impact.

The book was quite a few years old, however, when one day an agent for a German film producer arrived to say his client was interested in buying the film rights from the book.

I am still proud of myself that I thought and even said, "Let me ask our lawyer."

Believe it or not, we had acquired a lawyer when we signed deeds or mortgages pertaining to our farm. He was a very friendly Vermont old-timer who hadn't gone to law school but had learned the trade working in a law office in his youth. He was a very good friend of our own best friend in Stowe, "Uncle Craig," who brought us together.

Therefore, I presented the contract which the German firm had left with us to our lawyer. In this contract it said that the film company wanted to buy the book for $10,000, whereupon my lawyer advised me to ask for royalties.

The next time I was in New York I met the agent at the hotel and told him that we would like to receive $10,000 down payment and "X" percent of royalties.

I remember this situation as if it had happened yesterday. He looked at me long and thoughtfully and then said, "Permit me to call Germany. This I cannot decide on my own."

I was still so European that I was deeply impressed that somebody would, just like drinking a glass of water, place a long-distance call across the Atlantic Ocean.

In an incredibly short time he was back with a very sad face.

"I am sorry, I have to inform you that there is a law in existence which forbids a German film company from paying royalties to foreigners."

For a moment I felt funny to be called a foreigner. Then I realized that I was now an American citizen and therefore qualified as a foreigner to a German film company.

Unfortunately I took this information on face value instead of referring it to my lawyer to have it checked. I signed the contract.

In the contract the payment was due within a year. A few weeks after signing the contract I was called by the agent, who said if I agreed to take off 10 percent I could have the $9,000 immediately. He didn't even give me time to ask the family or the lawyer.

Well, we never—but really never—had any cash available. But we always had unpaid bills stacked up, so with a deep sigh I agreed. Two days later I received the check for $9,000.

Little did I know that with this I had signed away all film rights for the book. To put it in modern English, I had been taken.

Several years later an international contract lawyer informed me that I had been misinformed. There never was any such law existing in Germany, and I should have received royalties; but by this time it was too late.

The years had come and gone. We had stopped our concert work and I was deep in the jungle of New Guinea when some mail was forwarded to us at one of the major mission stations. As I came out of the jungle I looked through stacks and stacks of letters, among which was one where somebody said they were interested in making a musical out of my book, and that Mary Martin was supposed to play me. I didn't even read it through carefully before tearing it up. First of all, I couldn't visualize us on a theater stage; second, I didn't even know who Mary Martin was, and therefore was not duly impressed. I went back into the jungle for much more interesting and worthwhile work.

This happened again in Rabaul, and once more in Port Moresby. Every time the same type of letter. The third time I didn't even read it before tearing it up. I was getting impatient. What a silly idea.

Father Wasner and I had flown to New Guinea and the other South Sea Islands, but we returned on board ship. How Mary Martin's director ever found out about it, I shall never know; but as we docked in San Francisco, there they were—the agent and Mary Martin's husband, informing us that Mary was playing in

Annie Get Your Gun and that we would be guests of honor at the theater that same evening.

I remember how fully I enjoyed that performance and, when I met Mary Martin for the first time backstage, how genuine my hug and kiss were. I really felt that here was a great artist.

But at the same time I could not imagine that the one who played "Annie" could play me.

Weeks and months passed, during which time Rogers and Hammerstein and the famous Lindsey and Kraus who had written the best seller, *Life With Father,* were chosen to make a play from the book. In fact, they were all working on it already.

Then came the crux of the matter: the managers wanted not only the rights to the play but also the movie rights which I had already sold. So they had to turn to Germany and deal with the German movie people. There it was really revealed how I had sold myself away. Gloria Film in Munich had made the purchase, but they were completely uninterested as to whether I got anything out of this deal or not. Only because the American manager insisted that we participate at least in some small degree, I finally ended up getting three-eighths of 1 percent. At that time the Americans gambled on the venture, for no one knew how the play would be accepted or what the public would say and think. A great deal of money was sunk into the production.

After I had signed the contract, Mary Martin wanted to learn to know me; so she came up in the early summer to stay with us for ten days. At that time the Trapp Family Lodge boasted one room with bath, Room 28, which, of course was reserved for Mary. The other rooms shared a group of showers at the other end of the hall.

Mary was accompanied by her husband, who soon

had to go back to New York, and her director, who stayed on with her. Out of the corner of my eye for the next days I saw Mary imitating my long step and the way I talked vividly with my hands.

All of us enjoyed those ten days immensely. Mary Martin is such a warm womanly person, with no airs whatsoever. And she has a blessed sense of humor. Every now and then she shared with us something from her vast experiences on the stage and her travels. We usually rolled with laughter.

During those days I was allowed to make a few changes in the script, and I also taught her the Austrian folk dance, the *Landler*. For this help, I was given a special salary. Broadway behaved very nobly.

As the opening day came close, one day I received a huge package from Sak's Fifth Avenue. It was Mary's personal present to me, a beautiful pale green gown with matching pale green slippers, to be worn during opening night and afterward at a party. How very typical of this lovely person.

Then came the opening night. What excitement! There had been enough publicity, let alone the illustrious names of Mary Martin, Rogers and Hammerstein, Lindsey and Kraus to arouse the curiosity of everybody.

What I could not believe in San Francisco, I believed now: Mary Martin really portrayed me in all that young impetuousness. I was deeply touched, and I was the first one to jump to my feet. Then the whole house rose to a standing ovation for Mary Martin.

Backstage we were both congratulated and photographed together and asked for autographs, and quite a bit of time had passed before we left the theater.

On the street, friends of ours waited and shook my hand. Anong the many, many people was a young man who said, "Are you Mrs. von Trapp?"

When I said, "Yes," he put a piece of paper in my hand.

I said, "Thank you very much," and put it in my purse.

Later in the hotel as I looked in my purse, out fell that piece of paper. I read it but didn't quite understand it, so I showed it to Johannes and Father Wasner, who had been with me at the opening night. Father Wasner jumped up like he had been stung by a bumblebee.

I had been handed a subpoena. Of course, I had no idea what a subpoena was, so when I heard it was something legal I said, "Oh, let's go to the party first."

Arriving at the party in the big room on top of the St. Regis Hotel, I sensed an atmosphere of apprehension.

Finally someone whispered to me, "They are all waiting for the press to come out."

About an hour later Mary Martin came over to me and said, "Rogers is taking it much too seriously. I don't care if the newspapers say it is 'sweetie pie and gooey and entertainment for everybody from eight to twelve.' All of these nasty things that they have printed really do not bother me. I felt that the audience liked it, and I trust the people's taste."

The next years proved her right. No one seemed to have cared what the *New York Times*, the *Tribune*, etc., had said, and the *Sound of Music* was running on Broadway for four and a half years as one of the all-time successes.

Way past midnight and after a few very good waltzes I had danced, we finally returned to the hotel. Then I was reminded of the sober reality of the subpoena.

I simply couldn't believe it. Some man was insisting that I had appointed him as my agent and that he had arranged for *Sound of Music* to be put on stage! Now he was demanding $35,000!

We never had possessed so much money outright since we had arrived in America, and the whole story was simply outrageous. Not one word was true, but unfortunately I was forced to hire a lawyer in New York City. The case continued for years, with big bundles of information accumulated back and forth, and finally it came to court.

I was terribly excited. It was the first time in my life that I had been within a courthouse, and it was also the first time in my life that I was the accused. There were a good many other "firsts"—like the swearing in of the jury. I was getting more and more excited when the judge entered the room and everyone was rising. As he sat down, I suddenly saw on the white wall behind him—in big letters—"IN GOD WE TRUST."

That really helped me. I was so completely sure of my innocence that I didn't even doubt that the plaintiff would be proved to be a scoundrel in no time.

Then the big drama started. The prosecutor had the first word. As he started to tell his invented story, I jumped up time and again with hissing sounds like, "But this is not true!" or "I never did this," or "I never saw him in Los Angeles," until finally my lawyer turned around and really hushed me. He rolled his eyes at me and made it clear that I had to shut up and keep shut up. So with all my indignation and wrath I had to keep quiet while the other man was unrolling this great big stinking lie.

I noticed the judge looking at me a few times. I was just getting ready to jump up again when the judge got up and declared a recess.

Now I was hanging in midair, high and dry. I stormed out in the corridor with all the other people and went straight to my lawyer and said, "And why didn't you let me say anything? Not a word is true. And now there is a recess and he can think of new lies, and I don't understand a thing about anything anymore."

At that moment a gentleman nodded, approached our lawyer, and said something to him which made him raise his eyebrows. He turned to me and said, "This is a very rare thing. The bailiff just brought a message that the judge wants to see you, Mrs. von Trapp, in his chambers."

I came back to reality and said boldly, "OK, then I can tell him personally what I think of the whole thing."

Accompanied by Johannes, I went into the judge's chambers. As we entered he got up and came right over to me and said, "Mrs. von Trapp, I suggest a settlement of $3,000, and you will be rid of the whole story."

That hit me between the eyes.

"A—*what?*" And my eyes must have flashed fire. "But this man is a liar through and through, and I am completely innocent; he should pay his lawyer and mine like we do in Europe because he is wrong and I am right."

The judge looked at me very kindly and said, "I know, but if the jury doesn't think so it will be a hung jury. That means this can go on for years and years to come, and it will cost you more than $3,000 in the end."

I was completely dumbfounded. I could not grasp it.

"But look, Your Honor, behind your head it says, 'In God We Trust.'"

And the judge said very gently, "And that God in whom you trust, Mrs. von Trapp, sends you now His advice."

At that time Johannes took my arm and looked down at me. That big boy of mine really lovingly understood the qualms his mother was going through, but he also grasped much faster the truth of what the judge had said. Johannes said, "Mother, his Honor is right; take his advice."

At that moment I really felt somewhat solemn, like being touched by a messenger from God. So I said to the judge, "All right, I trust you." And then I made a mistake and added, "Mr. Honor." I was just too excited to get the words straight.

The bell rang. We all went back into the courtroom and the judge gave my lawyer a nod. He got up holding a ten-inch thick compilation of folders and papers in his left arm, turning pages and saying, "Mr. X, you met Mrs. von Trapp for the first time on July 19th. Is that true?"

Mr. X said, "Yes, that is true."

My lawyer turned the pages and then he said, "And then, Mr. X, you met Mrs. von Trapp on July 19th in Los Angeles for the first time—as you said under oath last winter."

And again pages were turned and my lawyer said, "But then, Mr. X, you met Mrs. von Trapp for the first time in Munich of the same year, as you said under oath on . . ., is that true?"

"Yes, that is correct."

Down came the gavel in the hand of the judge. He got up and, with a face I never would want to be turned against me, he said in the direction of Mr. X, "That is enough. I am empowered to suggest a settlement out of court for $3,000."

The lawyer of Mr. X jumped up and said, "Accepted. Accepted."

The judge said, "The case is closed."

With the Broadway people, everything had been out in the open. We had been informed of things ahead of time, and our opinion was asked. Our advice was requested, and most of the time it was taken. That produced a very friendly feeling of cooperation.

Not so with Hollywood! From then on we lived from rumors and hearsay. We "heard" that Twentieth Century Fox was going to make a film after the stage play.

The only thing I hadn't been quite happy about in the Broadway play was the portrayal of my husband, who had been made into a very strict disciplinarian, ruling his seven motherless children like a sea captain would his crew, while in fact he was the gentlest and kindest of fathers. That he called his children with a boatman's whistle was really because of practical reasons. Every one of us, me included, had his own signal, and the shrilling of that whistle could be heard for miles; so when we were in different sections of our big estate, the whistle would always find us.

On the stage the use of the whistle was a little bit overdone—giving the impression that our daily lives had been ruled and regulated by sharp whistle blasts. So when I heard about Hollywood's intention, I thought that this was my chance to do something about the false portrayal of my husband. So I tried to locate the producer. But it took months until I finally could speak to him on a person-to-person call from Stowe, Vermont, to Hollywood.

"Sir," I said, "I would very much like to talk about the portrayal of my husband, which I wasn't so very happy with on Broadway."

He interrupted me. "Oh, we are not concerned about persons and facts. I haven't read your book, and I don't intend to read it. We are more or less going to make our own version of your story."

I was horrified. "But," I explained, "you can't do that! We are not Napoleon; we are still alive."

"But we don't intend to make a documentary. This will be a musical."

"Sir," I pleaded, "don't get me wrong. I don't want to get any money out of this discussion. I would only like to tell you about my husband—how he really was."

Right away a little click told me that he had hung up. Never could I get him again.

Now I had time to really get excited. If they want to make their own story, I mused, what happens if they let me be divorced a couple of times? Or if they distort our family story and give the world a completely wrong impression of the Trapp family?

So as the months went by, my inner excitement mounted until I finally succeeded in making Twentieth Century Fox let me see a preview of the film. I was so relieved by what I saw that every time when I am asked (and that's many times a year), "And how do you like the film the *Sound of Music*? I still answer with that same old relief of that first viewing, "I really like it very much, especially the beginning where you can see beautiful Austria photographed from a helicopter. The pictures were taken from the air around Salzburg, and I could see this view every morning at breakfast."

I don't know why there was this invisible wall between us and the film people. By mere chance—just because I happened to come from Italy into Salzburg and found out that they were filming on the Cathedral Square—I went over and met the cast, including Julie Andrews, for a fleeting moment. But that was not intentional; otherwise we never would have met.

Thinking back on the opening night of the Broadway musical, I must have taken it for granted that I would be present at the first official showing of the premiere of the film. When I didn't hear anything about it and no invitation arrived, I really humbled myself to go and ask the producer whether I would be allowed to come. He said he was very sorry, indeed, but there was no seat left.

And that's the way it was, and that's the way it is. All the information I receive about the film is usually gotten from friends who send me clippings from newspapers, as I myself hardly ever read a newspaper. Somehow I feel sorry it is that way.

One thing turned into a kind of hardship. That was when the newspapers reported the film's phenomenal financial success which finally turned into a box-office record, even leaving behind *Gone with the Wind*. Unfortunately the people, not only in America but also in the rest of the world (the film has been shown literally all over the globe—to the last and newest African nation, to faraway South Sea Island tribes—just every where), simply think that we are rolling in the millions, and this accounts for the stacks of begging letters which I receive. Requests to build this, that and the other thing. The latest was to build a cemetery. I didn't know that a person could build a cemetery.

But, let me add quickly, that while we didn't become millionaires and all of us have always had to work hard for a living, *Sound of Music* has brought other blessings far beyond the reach of money!

Because of that one signature of the contract with the German film company in an unguarded and unprotected moment, I had signed all my rights away.

When the film was in the peak of its popularity, something happened which brought about a change in my life.

One day Johannes and I were in New York together. At that time I was still wearing my national Austrian dress; therefore, as we walked down the street, I stood out like a sore thumb.

At every street crossing, people would say, "Aren't you Mrs. Trapp?" and they'd shake my hand. Time and time again it made me miss the green light.

The worst came when Johannes took me to dinner that night. I hardly got around to eating because I had to sign so many autographs.

As we left the restaurant, Johannes whispered with emphasis, "Mother, if you want me to go anywhere with you again, change your clothes."

This wasn't quite that easy, for after twenty-seven years of wearing Austrian clothes, I was completely oblivious to American fashions.

Soon after that I was on a lecture tour again which brought me to Wright Patterson Air Force Base, where I talked to the officers' wives. After telling a couple of friends about my newfound plight, they eagerly offered to take me on a shopping spree to Dayton, Ohio.

There I had to change from top to bottom. Off went my comfortable dear "Hush Puppies," my red cotton stockings that I could wear for years, my comfortable bulky underwear, my long-skirted dress, the blouse with the handmade lace, and the brocade apron.

Instead I found myself balancing on high heels, looking suspiciously at those flimsy stockings, and feeling most uncomfortable in the short dress with my knees showing. All this was accompanied by the delighted oh's and ah's of my lady friends who thought I looked stunning.

Soon the time for Johannes to see his "new mother" arrived. I was waiting in the hotel lobby in my new regalia when Johannes came out of the elevator, walked over and with an astonished and happy smile and said, "Hello, Mother. Let's have lunch!"

First of all, while my family could hold it against me every single day of the year and more or less gently rub it in that they could now be sitting back and taking it easy instead of working hard, they have all forgiven me long, long, long ago. That alone is worth the experience of that fatal mistake.

But then there is the uncountable number of letters from all countries of the world, telling me that looking at the film *Sound of Music* has strengthened their trust in God, or has made them think for the first time in their life that God is Somebody who could be trusted.

" 'The most important thing in life is to find out what is the will of God, and then go and do it.' If it has turned out in the case of the Trapp Family so well and so successfully in their lives, maybe I'll try too." Letters like this make me fold my hands and say from the bottom of my heart, "Dear Lord, thank You for the *Sound of Music*."

19

Changing of the Guard

And then I got sick. I had had trouble with high blood pressure and was given pills to take daily—which I did. When I was in Europe on one of my buying trips for the gift shop, I happened to come to Innsbruck where I met my daughter Hedwig, who was teaching in a grade school high up in the Tirolean Alps.

When she saw me she said, "Mother, are you sick?"

I said, "No, why?"

"Look in the mirror. Your lips are purple."

"But I really don't feel sick," I said, "except I am tired—but anybody would be after such a trip."

"Mother, promise me to see a doctor this afternoon when you go back to Salzburg."

And because she was so urgent about it, I said lightheartedly, "I will."

As I returned to Salzburg I found in my hotel a most unexpected surprise: an invitation for a special reception given at the old palace for Queen Elizabeth of England.

There I was with my promise to Hedwig. I asked at the hotel for the name of a good heart specialist and then I went to see him.

He took one look at me and said, "How are you feeling?"

"I am tired out," I said. "That's all. But I have a

strenuous trip behind me, so that shouldn't be surprising. Otherwise I am all right."

After an electrocardiogram and more examination I was told that I had a severely overstrained heart. The doctor wanted me to go to the hospital right away.

I pleaded with him, "Look, the Queen of England comes only once into Austria and I happen to have this invitation. Can't you give me an injection or something to get me through this evening? I promise that tomorrow morning I will check in."

He yielded, and I got the injection and left. I had just time enough to buy a pair of very long white kid gloves to go with my beautiful light-blue evening gown. And then I sailed out to the reception.

This was really a gala performance. A very select guest list had been prepared from the first families in Salzburg. While I was standing there looking for someone whom I might know, people came over time and again, young couples, with the young ladies curtsying before me, introducing themselves as the sons and daughters of our old friends. It was like Vineta, the legend of the sunken city which comes out of the sea once every hundred years for one hour at midnight. All these illustrious names—counts, barons, dukes and princes—showed up, and I suddenly missed my husband most intensely.

Then the queen appeared and walked smilingly through the reception line, nodding to the left and to the right, and dinner was served. Sometime during the evening when she was finished with her dinner, the queen made the rounds, and all of us were introduced. I was still eating a most delicious dessert when a lady-in-waiting came over and said that Princess Anne had asked to see me. I tried to stick it out with my dessert and pleaded with the lady-in-waiting, "But, look, I am really not her generation. She doesn't have to be polite to me. Poor young princess—leave her alone."

But the lady-in-waiting insisted that it was the princess' personal wish. So with a farewell look at my only half-eaten Viennese specialty (I knew that the plate would be changed in my absence), I followed her into the next room. There Princess Anne really did want to see me and most eagerly wanted to find out whether the *Sound of Music,* which she had seen more than once in London, was a true story and if I was really the way the nuns sang, "How do you solve a problem like Maria?"

Finding refuge in a deep window protected by a floor-length brocade curtain, we chatted happily along. First we talked about the *Sound of Music,* then about myself and how I had been much worse than it was portrayed in the film, and finally about horseback riding and especially galloping. From where I stood I could see an anxious lady-in-waiting going around with searching eyes. Finally I had pity on her and told the princess that I had a sneaking suspicion she was being looked for, and we parted as great friends.

By that time it had become ten o'clock and the injection must have stopped working because suddenly I was really exhausted, and I couldn't stick it out. While no one was supposed to leave before the queen, I simply felt I had to go and lie down. One of my old friends helped me find a taxi and I went back to the hotel.

First thing the next morning, the telephone rang and the newspapers wanted a press conference. Again I learned something important the hard way: Never say no to the press.

I was really tired, it was only eight o'clock in the morning, and I said that I would be available later. And do you know what they did? The leading Salz-

burg newspaper said that I had had a nervous breakdown and couldn't receive the press. When I read that,
I could have cried.

A few hours later I checked into the hospital. News
had gotten out about this. In America, for instance, it
was in bold letters on the front pages: "Maria had a
heart attack." I began receiving telegrams from all
over the world—telegrams of sympathy and well wishing, which were very touching indeed.

Johannes was in the middle of his final examination
at Yale University to receive his degree in forestry
when he learned from the newspaper about what he
thought must be a severe sickness. It made him take
the next jet over to Salzburg.

I was resting in bed when there was a knock on the
door. I couldn't believe my eyes when Johannes was
standing there, life-size, with a big smile.

"How are you feeling, Mother?"

"I think right now I feel like a hundred million dollars," I answered. "What are you doing here? I
thought you were in your finals."

Then he told me about the newspapers. We spent a
wonderful weekend together. With the permission of
the doctor, he took me to Maria Plain, the old church
where the "Coronation Mass" by Mozart was being
performed on the very place for which it had been
composed when the old picture of the Madonna was
crowned with a jeweled crown.

Then I noticed that I was not altogether my old self;
I got tired very quickly.

The next morning Johannes said, "Mother, I had a
talk with the doctor, and he thinks you should not
work so hard and that all the excitement from running
the lodge is not good for you. Therefore, I suggest that
I take this off your shoulders and that you simply take
it easy."

I was overjoyed and agreed wholeheartedly. This was while I was still in the hospital and didn't feel too well.

When the doctor permitted me to leave the hospital, he had arranged a three-week stay at a place in the mountains, Kurhaus St. Joseph in Durrnberg bei Hallein, which has become a home away from home for me ever since.

The very fact that my youngest daughter came from America to help me on my return trip made me realize again that I must have been really sick. Lorli enjoyed being with me in Salzburg as much as I enjoyed being alone with her for the first time in many years. I was deeply touched and grateful.

When I returned home I tried to pick up where I had left off. In the meantime Johannes had looked around—especially at our books—and tried to get acquainted with the backstage of the hotel business. He was very astonished indeed when I acted like nothing had happened and nothing had been said. He had seen enough to realize that the Trapp Family Lodge had been run by an emotional mother who could never say no to employees who needed a strong hand, or to guests who pleaded they couldn't pay their bill due to sudden death or sickness in the family, which happened quite often. It was "now or never"—the lodge was so deep in the red that it was a question of survival.

"Mother, do you know what it means to be in the red?" Johannes asked.

"No, I have never heard this expression."

So Johannes explained to me the cold, hard facts. Then he reminded me about our talk in the hospital in Salzburg and added, "But if I have to take over, Mother, you will have to let go."

This was exactly it: How could I let go completely

with Johannes so young and inexperienced? Besides, he was newly married. I tenaciously held onto that very burden in order to do the guiding. For instance, I broke out in tears of pity when he wanted to fire somebody who needed badly to be fired.

Every so often Johannes would throw up his hands in utter dismay.

My aim while running the lodge had been to make the guests and the employees feel happy and content like one big family. Now I found Johannes brooding by the hour over sheets and sheets of figures. So I said it once too often, "But this is only money."

How often the family had heard me say that throughout the years! What I really had meant was that as long as we were together, how much more important this was than to have money.

But now Johannes tried to make me realize that there is a limit. If you don't have enough money to pay your debts and your bills, for a long period of time, you eventually may lose everything.

Months had passed by this time, with continual conflict back and forth between mother and son, and Christmas was now just around the corner.

One day Johannes said, "If I am running this place now, I would like so much to do it without the family at Christmas."

Impetuous as I am, I ventured, "How about Hedwig, Maria and I going skiing to Austria?"

Johannes jumped at it.

But again, I must not have really meant it because it dawned on me that on Christmas Eve I would not be downstairs in the living room with all the guests and the big Christmas tree with the many wax candles on it, but that I would be somewhere far away from home. I started whimpering, but this time Johannes remained adamant.

"Mother, you said so. Now let's leave it at that."

Under floods of tears and always quoting, "There was no room at the Inn," and feeling sorry for myself, we flew to Austria and went to the place where I had felt so much at home, Durrnberg bei Hallein. But, lo and behold, Durrnberg was closed until after Christmas. So off we went to a village in the Bavarian Alps where the parish priest is my most beloved of all pastors.

After the crying and the whimpering had been done and over with, we celebrated the most wonderful Christmas Eve. There were the two priests, Hedwig, Maria and I, all of us passionate singers. From seven o'clock until near midnight we kept singing Christmas motets and carols, without ever repeating, until we went over to midnight mass. The pastor whom I had known as a seminarian had turned into a wonderful parish priest who is able through his deep love and understanding to steer his parish of farmers and mountain people through the creeks and shallows of a changing church. It was an unforgettable Christmas for all of us.

Afterward we went to Durrnberg and spent a few more weeks there, and I really went skiing and enjoyed myself.

But still there was this thing in my heart and I felt like a dethroned queen.

When I returned home the situation hadn't changed much, except that now Johannes had really become suspicious. He had seen through the weeks that I really couldn't let go and would interfere in arrangements and changes, so he tried to be really stern. This brought more floods of tears from the side of his mother.

At that time I was advised by friends to find a lawyer who would keep me out of these emotional upsets, and I was extremely lucky in my choice. My lawyer became a friend to my family, and Johannes even asked him to become a director in our family corporation.

But I still hadn't learned to shut up. As Hemingway says, "It takes two years to learn a language and then it takes fifty years to learn to be silent."

Very quickly my lawyer sized up my personal situation and many times I had to hear his stern admonition: "Mrs. von Trapp, you have to learn to keep your mouth shut. In your time you have made your mistakes; now let him make his."

Finally I did what I should have done all along. In the utter despair of my heart I prayed to God for help. This was a year ago, and God had just waited for this sincere prayer in order to help me.

Like many other parents who have been leaders for a very long time, I simple didn't know how to step down without bitterness and reproaches, and without suspicion on my side that the next generation simply didn't know and didn't understand—

There I found myself in the middle of a generation gap. But I needed very special help, and God provided it in a very special way.

20

The New Pentecost

One day my daughter Maria gave me a book and said, "Mother, read this."

I took it to bed with me the same evening and finished it at 2:30 A.M. It was *The Cross and the Switchblade* by David Wilkerson.

Next morning I said to Maria, "That was marvelous —almost incredible!"

A few days later Maria gave me another book and it was almost as interesting. This time it was *Nine O'clock in the Morning* by Dennis L. Bennett. This I read in two sittings. When she asked me how I liked it, I said kind of nostalgically, "The faith of these people is really astounding, and so is the working of the Holy Spirit. But the first one is a Baptist, and the second one is an Episcopalian. Isn't the Holy Spirit working among us Catholics too?"

Maria just seemed to be waiting for this question, because she dashed into her room next to mine and returned with a yellow book, *The Pentecostal Movement in the Catholic Church* by Father O'Connor.

This was not quick reading. There was a lot of bone-dry theology to digest, but I devoured it hungrily.

When I had almost finished the "yellow book," the June 21 issue of *Time* magazine came out with a picture of Christ on the cover and a long article on the Jesus Movement. As I read it I came across a paragraph telling about the annual convention which the Catholic Pentecostals would have in the near future at Notre Dame University.

On the spur of the moment, this being "me," I called person to person to Notre Dame University to talk with Father O'Connor. That he was immediately on the line was a minor miracle, I was told later, because he is very hard to reach.

Eagerly I asked, "Father, I have just finished reading your book, and *Time* magazine tells me about the forthcoming convention at Notre Dame. Could somebody like me, who knows nothing about nothing, attend too, or is it just for the "in" people?"

"There will be many like you," he replied. "Come along. You are most welcome."

Spontaneously I called Holiday Inn in South Bend and reserved two single rooms "with air conditioning," and then I told Maria what I had done.

"Mother! Mother!" she exclaimed, hugging me.

Little did I know that months earlier my oldest daughter, Agatha, had been invited to a Catholic prayer meeting near Baltimore. It happens that as you read about it or watch it, a great longing arises in your soul and you find yourself seriously and sincerely praying that the Holy Spirit may come to you too. In due time she was, as it is called, "baptized in the Holy Spirit."

The eminent sensation of an overwhelming love and joy and peace filled her to overflowing, and immediately she thought of her sister Maria with whom she wanted to share this great experience. And so she invited her. Again, in due time, Maria was baptized in the Holy Spirit.

Now the two girls were wondering how in the world they could get their mother even near it. They knew I was very much opposed to private revelation, extraordinary happenings, appearances of the Madonna on

232

trees and housetops around the globe, etc. So for quite a few weeks they simply prayed over it. Then they decided to try via the books and were overjoyed when they saw the result.

Agatha and a friend, whom she helps in her kindergarten, left from Baltimore while Maria and I flew from Burlington. As we went into the airplane it was 60 degrees outside. Arriving in South Bend, it was 96 degrees—like a baking oven. The thought of the air-conditioned room for the night was a real consolation.

We arrived on Friday night, just in time for the opening of the convention which was being held in a big auditorium which was *not* air conditioned. With the temperature 96 degrees outside and with about 4,000 people inside, it surely was warm. On the platform sat a group of people. I was told they were the ones who five years earlier had started the Pentecostal movement in the Catholic Church simply by increasingly praying for the Holy Ghost to come. It started simultaneously at Notre Dame University in Indiana and Duquesne University in Pennsylvania, and in Ann Arbor, Michigan.

A Dominican sister, Sister Amata, was the mistress of ceremonies, and she called these believers forward one by one "to give witness."

I suffered a few shocks that first evening. One was from the very Protestant-sounding expressions, like "to give witness," or "to share with you," or what the ones who gave witness invariably report sooner or later of how they "accepted my Lord Jesus Christ as my personal Savior." Especially the latter expression irritated me greatly; I thought it was simply impertinent of a person to "accept Christ." Christ had come down to earth, lived among us, and died for us, and now I grandly "accept." It sounded unbearable to me.

The meeting started with singing, and between the

233

different "witnesses" there was more singing. There also was prayer, and then I heard a strange sound. People were praying half aloud but not in English. Behind me were different sounds. Some very enthusiastic girls were simply saying, "La-la-la-la." That was very strange.

Once more Sister Amata got up and said, "Now let me introduce to you, Jim Cavnar."

A tall slender young man with dark hair and a big smile stepped forward and said, "It gives me great honor and great pleasure to introduce to you my father, Colonel Cavnar."

From the background rose a gentleman—every inch an officer. With firm steps he marched forward to the microphone. He stood ramrod straight, with the same big smile as his son Jim.

"Until recently I was a colonel in the United States Air Force," he began. "In my days I was the most decorated officer. Being a Catholic, I sent my children to a Catholic school. So it happened that my son Jim landed at Notre Dame. When he was in his last year of college I had business that brought me near South Bend one day, and I thought I would have a look at Jim. But he was not in his room. When I asked his colleagues about him, they said, 'Jim is praying.'

" 'Jim is *what?*' I exclaimed.

" 'Jim is praying,' they repeated. 'Jim is always praying.'

"I went in search of Jim. Sure enough, I found him in one of the chapels. I beckoned him to come outside and said, 'Son, what's going on? Today is Wednesday. Do you have a special holy day here today?'

" 'No, father,' said Jim.

" 'But why are you praying on Wednesday afternoon?' I inquired, slightly impatient.

" 'Well, Father, there is so much to pray for.'

234

" 'Son,' I said, 'I sent you here for your academic studies and for football. But not for praying on Wednesday afternoon, mind you.'

"Jim was very polite, but I saw right away that I hadn't stopped him from praying on Wednesday afternoon—or any other afternoon, for that matter.

"Soon afterward Jim graduated Summa Cum Laude and got the most outstanding offers from different businesses, and also scholarships from leading universities in the country. And what did Jim do? He started a 'House of Prayer.'

"Well, I can tell you there is no money in a house of prayer, and I was really quite upset. I was a bitter father. The letter I sent to Notre Dame I know they would not frame. But what could I do? Jim was past twenty-one.

"About a year later I received an invitation to Jim's wedding. Now I was really bewildered. In his house of prayer he hardly made enough to live by himself. Now he was going to have a wife and eventually some children. So I went to that wedding a little ahead of time and went straight to the church. I didn't want to meet anybody. I didn't want to be talked to. I didn't want to be asked questions. I simply wanted to get it over with.

"Finally the wedding procession began, the nuptial mass got under way, and it came time for communion. With many other people I went to the front to the altar and, as I received Holy Communion, our Lord hit me on the head." (This is how Colonel Cavnar told it. We learned later from Jim that his father was enveloped in a blinding light almost like Saint Paul on his way to Damascus.)

"After the service I went up to my son, knelt down, and said, 'Jim, please pray over me. I want to receive the Holy Spirit.'

"Jim did, and the Holy Spirit filled my heart.

"Only later did I learn what Jim was praying for on that famous Wednesday afternoon—and before and after—it was for the very moment when his father would 'see the light.'

"And life has never been the same again."

I still remember how with his last words the colonel's voice sounded a little choked. We were all deeply moved. It was the highlight of the evening for me, and it kindled the fire of longing in my heart. As I had read in the "yellow book," it was the custom that at the end of such a national convention of the Pentecostal movement, newcomers who wish to receive the Holy Spirit would step forward and ask to be prayed over. As I went with the girls over to the Holiday Inn on the first evening, I resolved in my heart that this was what I was going to do.

The next day was Saturday. We had been given a timetable of the schedule between Friday evening and Sunday afternoon. Saturday was the day of the workshops; there were three. One was at 10:00 A.M., one at 1:30 P.M. and one at 7:30 P.M. The schedule said that those who aspired to receive the Holy Spirit should attend a certain workshop. So after breakfast I cheerily said "Good-bye" to my girls, who would attend different workshops, and wound my way across the campus looking for the class building which would house my workshop.

And then something funny happened. As I walked along I heard cheerful shouting all across the campus: "Praise the Lord! Praise the Lord!"

As this went on, it began to get on my nerves.

"Can't these people say 'good morning' like other good Christians?" I mumbled to myself. *And that la-la-la-la business last night,* I kept thinking, *is not a must.*

Finally I found my classroom in one of the old buildings on the campus. It was half full already I didn't know anybody. Some of these people struck me as very, very starry-eyed, and again, "Praise the Lord! Praise the Lord!" could be heard all over the big room.

Finally the session started. It was hot. The gentleman who talked had a very monotonous voice and no microphone. It was strenuous to follow him. The subject matter was the most basic teaching on the Holy Spirit, His seven gifts, His twelve fruits, and what every Catholic child learns in catechism class before receiving the sacrament of confirmation.

After forty-five minutes there was a short interval where we stretched our legs, and then we listened to "Witnesses." Among others, there was a mother-daughter team, and I remember that they were the ones who had struck me as being so very starry-eyed. They described what a sinful life they had lived previously, and how sinful it was in every detail, and how the Holy Spirit had finally cured them from their sin.

I was getting increasingly more irritated. *Is this what all this is about?* I kept asking myself. Maybe this is not for me.

Then there was another intermission in which we all went outside and sat down on the grass. Next came a question-and-answer period. The very first question was: "What is speaking in tongues all about?"

I pricked up my ears. That was the one question which interested me above all else.

A dear elderly sister took it upon herself to answer. "Well, that is quite something," she said. "First you feel something building up in your stomach, and then it comes up and up and up, and suddenly you spit it out and there you are talking in tongues."

This was accompanied by descriptive gestures and faces.

I had had it! Now I was sure this was not for me. Agatha and Maria were already waiting for me.

"How did you like it, Mother?" they asked eagerly and most expectantly.

I felt bitterly sorry because I had to say, "Not at all —not at all. I don't think I should stay here." Then I told them about my mixed feelings.

Maria came to my rescue. "You know what, Mother?" she said. "Now you have been through your session once. This afternoon you should come with me to mine. I tell you, in all my life I haven't heard anything so moving and so compelling about the spiritual life as in that hour."

So I got some new hope, and after lunch I set out with Maria to her workshop in a theater. It was after lunch, and it was getting hotter. Everybody was a little tired, and so was the speaker. I didn't hear anything so earthshakingly special.

After a little while, Maria turned to me and said a little embarrassed, "But he was so much better this morning."

The time passed, and I became more and more convinced that it was not the thing for me and I would not stay. But I didn't want to hurt the girls, and I didn't want to spoil their pleasure. They obviously were enjoying themselves immensely. On the other hand, I knew I would feel like a phony if I stayed one hour longer than absolutely necessary. And "absolutely necessary" meant I would stay through dinner and, while the others were going to their last workshop, I would simply leave quietly all by myself. After I had made up my mind to do this, a certain calm settled down on me. But it was not peaceful.

There was one more thing I wanted to do before

leaving: go to the grave of Sister Madleva. For many years she had been president of St. Mary's College, and it was she who had handed me my scroll for my honorary Ph.D. Her famous poems had brought light and happiness into many people's lives. For many years we had been pen friends. So I asked my way to the cemetery behind the college grounds. As I stood at her graveside, I felt very lonesome for her; she would have understood my bewilderment.

As I turned slowly away, my eye caught a large statue partly hidden by trees. It was Mary, standing there on a rock, her arms outstretched, smiling down at me.

I stood there for a little while and gazed at her. Then I simply said, "Oh, Maria, *hilf!*" ((You will always do praying and counting in your mother tongue. "Oh, Mary, Help!")

There was my mother to whom I had turned so many times in my life, as all children do in critical situations. While my mind was still set on getting out as soon as possible, all of a sudden I felt less tense—as if things would turn out all right after all.

As I was walking across the campus on the way to the car in order to go to the Holiday Inn for dinner, I met Sister Amata.

She stopped and asked, "How are you, Mrs. von Trapp?"

"Could be worse, Sister, but not much," I answered truthfully.

"Then I have to pray even harder," she replied, and she gave me a meaningful look. (On the next day when I met her again, she told me that she was almost scared—so strongly did she feel the presence of evil spirits working on me.)

While the others were parking the car, I ran ahead because on the way to the dining room I knew we had to pass the desk. I asked the lady at the desk, "When is the next plane leaving?"

"Where to?" she asked.

"Never mind," I blurted out. "Just leaving."

"Well, I will have to call the airport, so why don't you have dinner and I will find out."

Hastily I said, "Never mind about finding out. Book a seat on the next plane out of South Bend, *please*."

With this, my girls had just caught up with me, and together we went into the dining room.

It was a very polite dinner conversation, and it seemed endless to me. As we were finishing, Agatha suddenly said, "Here is Jim."

Jim Cavnar was passing our table, and I hurried after him and asked, "Jim, is your father still here or has he left already?"

"No, he is still here," said Jim. "In fact, he is coming now."

As I turned around, there was the colonel. He strode right over to me, arms outstretched, and said, "Maria, I was so looking forward to meeting you personally. We have read your books over and over again in our family, and I want to thank you very much for many wonderful hours. Are you enjoying it here?"

There was the question I had dreaded. But truthfully I said, "I'm sorry—not at all. In fact, I know now that I shouldn't stay here any longer, and I have just made arrangements to leave on the next airplane. You know, I am really disappointed. In the book Father O'Connor said, 'Anybody who is aspiring to be baptized in the Holy Spirit should say so in the end of the session.' But I was told this year that you don't do it anymore, and this was the big reason why I came."

"Oh, don't worry, Maria. We just don't do it in public anymore because it was misused in other years. But we will be only too happy to pray over anybody

240

who is ready to receive the Holy Spirit. In fact, I *wanted* you to come to our apartment right after the next workshop."

He gave me the number of his apartment, which was close to our rooms. Then he looked at his watch and said, "But, my, I'm late already. See you soon."

And off he rushed, leaving me behind—more bewildered than ever. My plans were shattered. I knew I couldn't run away now.

As I passed the desk, I said to the lady, "Thank you very much, but forget it. I'm not leaving." (And to this very day and hour I am angry at myself that I hadn't inquired where I would have gone. Maybe to Mexico? The West Coast? Canada?)

Very slowly and thoughtfully I wound my way to where I had heard my girls were going: Father O'Connor's workshop on the discernment of spirits.

A very large crowd had assembled, and I was amazed that Agatha and Maria found me. I could almost feel their great relief at seeing me again, because I had avoided a straight answer to the question of which workshop I was going to.

It turned out to be an especially good talk of one hour's duration, with an extremely good question-and-answer period.

While I listened to what was going on, thoughts went storming through my mind. From what I had learned about the baptism of the Holy Spirit, it made me wonder about our sacrament of confirmation and what had become of it. In Catholic Austria, confirmation means a new wristwatch, a trip to a famous amusement park, a good dinner, and somewhere sandwiched in the middle—church—"But it won't take too long." It's memorizing seven gifts, twelve fruits, fuss about a sponsor and a name, and trying to remember why the bishop is going to tap your cheek, and wondering what it's going to feel like.

Baptism in the Holy Spirit must have been the sacrament of confirmation for the first Christians, I mused.

Then I analyzed how we grow up now. We're baptized as babies, and our godparents mumble something we don't understand. We have our first confession full of fear, and our first communion full of reverence. Somehow, somewhere, Jesus is all mixed up in this, but many of us never clearly, in words, acknowledge Him as our personal Savior. We may go to daily communion all our lives and yet never have met Him as a person!

In Revelation 3:20-22 we read, "Behold, I stand at the door and knock; if any one hears My voice and opens the door, I will come in to him, and will dine with him, and he with Me."

How I thank God that I too realized that need for a personal commitment. And that morning I did just that!

This invitation to Him is there in many of our lives, but not consciously enough. We need to awaken to Him and make a *personal* person-to-person commitment. One of the things the Holy Spirit is doing in the charismatic renewal is lifting a veil that has kept many Catholics from the personal relationship with Jesus that is there for the asking.

The most interesting part of Father O'Connor's talk was when he told about the battle in which we are directly involved—the battle of the Holy Spirit and the unholy spirit, namely, the Spirit of God and the satanic powers, and how it was Satan's greatest triumph to have gotten so many modern Christians and theologians to pooh-pooh the reality of evil spirits.

I recalled right away how several times I had been

accosted by visiting priests, usually young ones, who would say in an incredulous tone, "But, Baroness, you don't mean it. You don't really believe in angels and devils anymore. These are old legends . . . ."

This is Satan's great alibi.

After a short interval in which we all took a brief recess, we sat down again and I attended my first real prayer meeting. There were singing and praying, listening to others pray in tongues, and later, singing in tongues. The Scripture reading was followed by silence and then more prayers and what I was told were called prophecies. My overall impression was slight bewilderment, but it left me with a truly reverent feeling. When it was all over Father O'Connor said, "God bless you and good night."

And now—this was the hour. I said good night to Agatha and her friend, and asked Maria to come along with me. On the way over I told her what had happened, and with that we arrived at Colonel Cavnar's apartment. As we entered, Maria was ushered to a neighboring room and I was left alone with a young man whom I had seen the night before on the platform. He interrogated me now on the teaching of the Holy Spirit. It was quite a thorough examination, but thanks to having studied Father O'Connor's book and afterward having read the Acts of the apostles and the passages of the epistles referring to the Holy Spirit, I passed the test and was pronounced "ready."

Then we went into the other room where Maria was waiting with Colonel Cavnar and a few other people. I knelt down and Colonel Cavnar placed his hands on my head while the others put theirs on my shoulders. First everybody prayed quietly, and then the colonel prayed out loud. How that man can pray! With such conviction, with such faith.

"Jesus, You said, 'Where there are two or three in

243

my name, I am in their midst.' We believe firmly that You are here with us in this room. You also said, 'Whatever you will ask the heavenly Father in my name, it will be given to you.' We ask now on behalf of our sister Maria who aspires to be filled with the Holy Spirit. She is longing, and we think she is ready. Come, Holy Spirit. Come."

I had never heard a grown-up man pray like this. He went on for a few minutes, and then they all prayed in their own tongue.

During the interrogation I had said timidly, "I talk English and German perfectly. Could I please ask the Holy Spirit to let that be enough? I really don't want anything to do with tongues."

And I had repeated this in the other room to the colonel. With great kindness and patience, he looked at me and said, "Maria, if God wanted something that would be real hard for you to give, maybe even your life, I am pretty sure you wouldn't say no. So don't be fussy now about speaking in tongues. If the Holy Spirit wants to give it to you, take it."

To this I couldn't say no.

Somebody at that moment uttered a prophecy which Maria said afterward was very beautiful. I, however, was in such deep reflection that I didn't even hear it.

After a little while the colonel looked at me and said, "Maria, say it."

"Say what?" I asked.

"I see syllables form on your lips. Say them."

"What syllables—do, re, me?."

A little impatient: "No, not 'do, re, me.' "

"But, what then? Alleluja?"

"Not alleluja. Just say what is coming."

Maria told me later that then I uttered some beautiful, very melodious words, which again I do not remember. Next we all praised God, and everybody hugged me. By then it was way after midnight, and we all said good night.

As I said good night to Maria and went to my own room, I must have expected something to happen because I remember I was astonished that going to bed was just like any other day—taking a shower, brushing my teeth, putting on my muumuu, and getting into bed. What had I expected? Floating through the room? Hearing things? Seeing things? Well—I turned out my light because I was really tired, "happily tired."

But the next morning! What a change! As I opened my eyes I was so filled with a tremendous love—love to God and to everybody on earth—my own dear ones and also people known and unknown—just love! Such deep peace and joy I had never felt before. Quickly I got up and dressed. I was in dire need for someone to hug. To open my arms wide. Thank God, Maria was next door. I rushed to her room and all I could repeat over and over again was, strangely enough, "Praise the Lord! Praise the Lord!"

I remember when I looked at the schedule on that very first Friday evening and noticed that on Sunday the community mass would be said in the big stadium and would last for three hours. I immediately resolved, "I will have to make a few telephone calls within that time because I can't possibly pray three hours nonstop."

As the colonel had said in his unforgettable talk, "Life has never been the same again."

I was experiencing that already.

One thing which happened to me almost immediately was that I felt eagerly drawn to search the pages of the New Testament throughout the Acts of the

apostles and the letters of Saint Paul, and through all
the passages which dealt with the Holy Spirit. I was
amazed at what I read. I had read the Bible most of
my grown-up life. But when I read the very same
pages now, they sounded so completely different and I
clutched the little pocket New Testament and in walking up and down stairs and crossing the campus, I
couldn't help but snatch a few more lines here and
there. That stayed with me. Now I am getting up an
hour earlier to be sure to have time for reading the
Scriptures before my working day begins. And every
day it is like stepping up to a table heavily laden with
delicious foods chosen for my needs. We all began to
get ready for Sunday Mass. As we had to drive from
Holiday Inn to Notre Dame, we went early enough to
get a good parking place. This way we were among
the first ones in this tremendously big stadium and
were able to take it all in as the thousands of people
—over 6,000—came eagerly strolling in. Singing started
in a most joyful and kind of preparatory way
in different sections, and was picked up by the others.
Then a sign was given and silence fell over the big
crowd as the procession of the priests began to file in;
160 priests were concelebrating with two bishops.

Three hours later when the last word was said,
"The mass is ended; go in peace," nobody could believe it. Where had the three hours gone? It had been
a wonderful time of praying together, singing together,
listening to prophecies, listening to prayer in tongues,
listening to the Holy Scriptures, and listening to the
beautiful sermon which Bishop A preached until it
was time for Bishop B to start the holy sacrifice. Finally seventeen priests had assisted with giving Holy
Communion. The people had come down the amphi-
theater aisles, and the hall was filled with happy song.

Nobody wanted to leave. We couldn't tear ourselves

away. Smaller and bigger groups were hanging around outside for the last farewell and to rejoice with "Praise the Lord."

The new Pentecost for which Pope John XXIII had prayed so fervently at the opening of the Second Vatican Council had happened to all of us right there. One noticed it most in the spirit of genuine love. This was not starry-eyed emotionalism; this was the true thing. Men embracing men with a wish of peace, *shalom,* God bless and keep you. Everybody showing his love and happy understanding to everyone else. There were no more strangers. If there had been outsiders from the "world," they would have said like in the first days: "Look at them, how they love one another. They are one heart and one soul. *Cor Unum et Anima Una!*"

As our return flight was on Monday, the next day, we had some more precious hours together "in spirit." After dinner we were invited to Colonel Cavnar's apartment again, and there was some more singing and, most important of all, more prayer.

Merely by listening to the prayer, we learned how to treat Jesus as our older brother with whom we together approach the heavenly Father "in His name." We also learned how to pray for each other's needs, and how to take "whatsoever you ask" literally. Things one would have never dared before to mention in prayer—everything—was laid before the eyes of God. Nothing was unimportant. Just like Jesus had said, "The heavenly Father knows the number of hairs on your head, and not one sparrow falls from the tree without His knowing." How much more everything concerning us, His dear children!

It was a new and altogether wonderful science to learn how to pray.

I must confess that time and again I had to over-

247

come some little embarrassment. We Catholics were simply not trained to pray right out loud and out in the open. We grew up with our liturgical prayers which, translated from Latin, were very formal. The ones among us who had picked up meditation during retreats had learned to talk to God in a personal way, but for heaven's sake not out loud in front of anybody else; it was my very own private affair between God and me. It needed some getting used to. But once the barrier was broken, it was most heartwarming to loudly and distinctly acknowledge His presence in our midst. Truly the new Pentecost is here.

21

Another New Beginning

And then I returned home.

For two blessed weeks, fourteen days and nights, I was steeped as it were in this deep pervading peace, love and joy, and nothing could disturb it. It was really that peace of which Jesus said, "As the world cannot give it." And one could add, "And the world cannot take it away either."

Nothing would get on my nerves. People and things which I knew from experience would irritate me, did not irritate me in the least. It was just a foretaste of heaven. But it was nothing unreal; I did not live on a cloud. I was right back in my daily work in our very busy lodge with hundreds of people coming every day, passing through our gift shop, with me giving autographs and being photographed just like always in the summer—except it was different.

While certain days, with the crowds milling through the gift shop, seemed to be endless and I began to get tired around four o'clock in the afternoon, that peace deep down in the soul was never disturbed. Smiling might become a little difficult and I might feel somewhat wilted after having been photographed more than the hundredth time, but I remembered vividly that while it was for me the "one hundredth time," it was for the person who took the picture the "one time," the moment they had come for from Arkansas,

Louisiana, Mississippi, anywhere in the Midwest, Seattle, and even Hawaii. While in other summers I never thought that far and simply got nervous and tired and impatient, this summer I was often amazed that at the very end of the day I was still genuinely obliging and friendly. In fact, if it made me feel anything, it made me feel humble that the people would take all that trouble to travel for many hundreds of miles just to shake my hand and take my picture. I attribute this to the person of the Holy Spirit that I did not get annoyed or frusrated.

The light and the glory of the wonderful prayer meeting at Notre Dame University were still with me. Then I found out that there were other small groups around that also held prayer meetings, and I was really longing to join them as soon as possible and as often as I could. While the prayer meetings usually started with a prayer, being almost always followed by everybody praying in tongues, most of the time was devoted to people "giving witness" or to people "sharing." Then I learned a new word; people were giving *prophecies*. All this seemed to be very important, but it left me cold and empty; there was so little praying done. I got more and more depressed because many a time this or that person simply seemed to use the opportunity to talk, talk, talk. More often than not, I used to come home not elated like I had been at Notre Dame, but disappointed or even downcast.

Then the Holy Spirit came to my help. Maria and I were invited to Ann Arbor, Michigan, to spend five days there with a group of people who had been baptized in the Holy spirit and were now simply living their life as had the first Christians. They are all working people. Some are busy at the university, either as students or teachers, and one is a dean. Others are working in offices. There are housewives with little children. The whole big group of six or seven hundred is truly living according to the gospels; the ones who have enough give to the ones who don't have enough, and all have sufficient. This is done very naturally and inconspicuously.

While we were there a young friend whom we had met in Notre Dame had told us upon our arrival that she was expecting her second child. Exactly two days later, her labor began and she lost the child. We witnessed how a heavy cross was made lighter by the love and concern and prayer of all. This deep peace, love and joy which I had learned to know, prevailed through those days, and again I remembered the words from the Acts of the apostles: "Look at them, how they love one another."

Those five days in their midst and the two prayer meetings, one on Monday and one on Thursday, strengthened and reinforced my spirit. From the manner in which the prayer meetings are conducted, I learned that prayer is the mainstay of a prayer meeting and that there may be periods of silent prayer. Leaders are necessary because, human nature being what it is, talk for talk's sake might creep in.

That time in Ann Arbor was a real retreat for me, and I had a lot of time to think. One thing became very clear, and since then I have felt much better.

The new Pentecost for which our saintly Pope John had prayed so fervently is really descending upon our earth. Not only upon Catholics and Protestants, but on all of God's children, as is evident as we learn of the happenings in Indonesia, in some parts of Africa, India, Pakistan and the South Sea Islands, and in our own America with its Jesus Revolution. Consequently, Satan and his evil spirits cannot be idle. He cannot let all of this happen without trying to destroy it. Therefore, he is simply making use of our human nature and creeping into the prayer meetings and making them religious socials; he makes the side issues, like praying in tongues or uttering prophecies, become the most important thing. Thus he gets the extraordinary into the foreground, as he does in spiritism and other occults. With the Holy Spirit making such tremendous headway all over the world, it should be self-explanatory to us that Satan and his evil spirits cannot be idle. But all we have to do is be careful and to listen to what St. Paul experienced on that very same thing in 1 Corinthians 12:27-31.

In the very early days St. Paul must have experienced a similar situation, because he warned the Christians, telling them there are different gifts and different people, but not all are called upon to do the same thing. And then he said, with great emphasis, in 1 Corinthians 12:31–13:13, "But earnestly desire the greater gifts. And I show you a still more excellent way.

"If I speak with the tongues of men and of angels, but do not have love, I have become a noisy gong or a clanging cymbal.

"And if I have the gift of prophecy, and know all mysteries and all knowledge; and if I have all faith, so as to remove mountains, but do not have love, I am nothing.

"Love is patient, love is kind, and is not jealous; love does not brag and is not arrogant, does not act unbecomingly, does not rejoice in unrighteousness, but rejoices with the truth.

"Love never fails; but if there are gifts of prophecy, they will be done away; if there are tongues, they will cease; if there is knowledge, it will be done away."

There are three things in the end that last, "but the greatest of these is love."

Where were these insurmountable obstacles between my son and myself? Much of it I found childish and ridiculous on my part. Of course I had to do it his way. All of a sudden it wasn't a bit difficult anymore to stop running the show. It all fell into place.

And as I relaxed I found myself with a lot of time on my hands—time for traveling around and visiting my family.

For more than twenty years I had been a grandmother. But I was not a "practicing grandmother," partly because I was really extremely busy, but partly for another reason. As my children got married I made up my mind never to be a *mother-in-law* in the proverbial sense of the word. Too long I had been accused of having been a domineering mother, so it was my iron resolution that this would not continue into the next generation. Unfortunately, with my tendency to exaggerate, I practically didn't go near the young couples in order to "leave them alone." I just left them alone too much. Children were born and suddenly began to go to school, and I hardly knew them. The last week in June is "Family Week," which now is the time for me to find out "how much they have grown."

As I look back over my life I see two great obvious mistakes. First, I tried so desperately hard never to give my husband's children the impression that I was their stepmother that I hardly dared to take care of my own babies as they came along. I left them mostly to their older sisters while depriving them of a true mother's love. Years later I made the same mistake all over again with the grandchildren. Now I hope I have awakened in time.

Weeks and months have passed. New confidence is building up on all sides, and "life has never been the same again."